D0484367

RENEWALS 458-4574

DATE DUE

WITHDRAWN
UTSA LIBRARIES

Reinventing the CFO

Other Books by Coopers & Lybrand

BEST PRACTICES IN REENGINEERING: WHAT WORKS AND WHAT DOESN'T IN THE
REENGINEERING PROCESS
Henry Johansson and David Carr

Reinventing the CFO

Moving from Financial Management to Strategic Management

Thomas Walther

Henry Johansson

John Dunleavy

Elizabeth Hjelm

Coopers & Lybrand

McGraw-Hill

New York   San Francisco   Washington, D.C.   Auckland   Bogotá
Caracas   Lisbon   London   Madrid   Mexico City   Milan
Montreal   New Delhi   San Juan   Singapore
Sydney   Tokyo   Toronto

Library of Congress Cataloging-in-Publication Data

Reinventing the CFO : moving from financial management to strategic
    management / Henry Johansson...[et al.].
        p.   cm.
    Includes bibliographical references and index.
    ISBN 0-07-012945-2 (hard : alk. paper)
    1. Chief financial officers.   2. Strategic planning.
3. Corporations—Finance.   I. Johansson, Henry J.
HG4027.35.R45   1996
    658.15—dc20   96-31878
                                                                           CIP

McGraw-Hill

A Division of The McGraw·Hill Companies

Copyright © 1997 by The McGraw-Hill Companies, Inc. All rights
reserved. Printed in the United States of America. Except as permitted
under the United States Copyright Act of 1976, no part of this publication
may be reproduced or distributed in any form or by any means, or stored
in a data base or retrieval system, without the prior written permission of
the publisher.

1 2 3 4 5 6 7 8 9 0   BKP/BKP   9 0 1 0 9 8 7 6

ISBN 0-07-012945-2

*The sponsoring editor for this book was Susan Barry, the editing supervisor
was Penny Linskey, and the production supervisor was Pamela Pelton. It was
set in Palatino by Victoria Khavkina of McGraw-Hill's Professional Book
Group composition unit.*

Printed and bound by Quebecor/Book Press.

McGraw-Hill books are available at special quantity discounts to use as
premiums and sales promotions, or for use in corporate training programs. For more information, please write to the Director of Special Sales,
McGraw-Hill, 11 West 19th Street, New York, NY 10011. Or contact your
local bookstore.

This book is printed on acid-free paper.

Information contained in this work has been obtained by The
McGraw-Hill Companies, Inc. ("McGraw-Hill") from sources
believed to be reliable. However, neither McGraw-Hill nor its
authors guarantees the accuracy or completeness of any information published herein and neither McGraw-Hill nor its authors shall
be responsible for any errors, omissions, or damages arising out of
use of this information. This work is published with the understanding that McGraw-Hill and its authors are supplying information, but are not attempting to render engineering or other professional services. If such services are required, the assistance of an
appropriate professional should be sought.

Library
University of Texas
at San Antonio

To Len Olin, our partner and friend

Contents

Foreword

For two decades now, management theorists, consultants, and practitioners all have been looking for ways to reawaken corporate earnings, productivity and overall competitiveness. Despite their best efforts, many undertakings have fallen flat.

Time and time again, when asked why these efforts seem futile, they raise the cry, "The accountants are killing us!"

We in the finance profession have been loath to hear their lament. But we need to open our ears, and open our minds to the possibility of a new relationship between the finance arm of a corporation and the marketing and operations arms.

We can no longer fall back on our old response, "we're only doing our job; being the guardians of the corporation's fiduciary responsibility to our shareholders."

Tom Walther, Hank Johansson, Jack Dunleavy, and Beth Hjelm have done us a real service with their book. They have given us in the finance profession—from multinational CFOs to accounts payable personnel at a one-factory company—a framework with which we can begin transforming ourselves as individuals and transforming our finance organizations into 21st century corporate partners.

The transformation of the Office of the Chief Financial Officer—from a position of being the financial cop to one of being the strategic coordinator of such actions as establishing an appropriate risk profile for a company, developing a worthwhile customer costing process that marketing managers can use, and most of all becoming a full "business" partner within the corporation's executive suite—is complex and frought with danger for those who take it on unprepared.

It is imperative that we in the finance organization realize that this transformation is not just about automating activities, or about reducing steps in our processes, or about reducing personnel. It is about becoming forward looking, rather than backward checking. It is about providing our colleagues in the top level of corporate management with "down-field vision" as they engage in strategic and tactical decision making. Most of all, it is about changing the way each and every individual within a corporation's finance organization thinks about his or her role.

To make this transformation happen requires from those who lead finance organizations a host of management and "people" skills many of us did not receive as part of our education or training, as well as traditional finance and accounting skills. It requires, in many instances, that we work against our natural strengths, for which we self-selected the finance field and for which we have been rewarded and promoted for a generation or more. It requires firmness of resolve and a healthy dose of impatience, tempered with humanity for both those who simply cannot perform in the new world and for those who are making huge changes in their own behavior in order to do so.

I am fortunate to have spent a number of years as a colleague of the author's at Coopers & Lybrand, and I and my clients profited mightily from their thoughtfulness and their expertise when undertaking the kinds of transformations they describe here. I am especially fortunate that when I left C&L to take my present position I was able to take a pre-publication copy of this manuscript with me.

This book is serving me and my colleagues as a blueprint for change as we enter the arduous task of making over our OCFO in order to help our company compete, excel, and lead in the 21st century. I'm sure it can do the same for you and your colleagues, both within your finance organization and within other disciplines with which you need to become a business partner in the future.

Read and take the message to heart. Remember, the future is here today, and it belongs to those brave enough to reach out and grasp it.

Michael Glinsky
Chief Financial Officer, U.S. West

Acknowledgments

Yes, we are accountants! Even after completing this manuscript that deals with the challenges facing Finance and Accounting organizations around the world, we are still accountants at heart. We have seen this profession change dramatically over the last decade, not only as practitioners ourselves but in our clients. And as the changes our clients are addressing have emerged, we, too, have gotten a "wake–up call" to change our own activities and develop a coherent framework that addresses the changes which we have observed.

While there are four names on the cover of this book, there are in fact many individuals who have been instrumental in the development of the Office of the CFO framework as well as in its application to client organizations around the world. For more than three years we have hosted CFO Forums in numerous cities where more than 300 CFOs from many different industries come together to discuss their rapidly changing roles and responsibilities. The rich dialogue and active participation in these CFO Forums has provided us with an invaluable learning experience.

Three of our former colleagues were instrumental as we began to work on these issues. Jeff Liss, Bob Lage, and Steve Wood helped define the early foundation for the Office of the CFO framework as the supporting methodologies and tools. We miss them and their intellectual contributions. Throughout the last four years, we were pushed and prodded by several key clients and academics. Most notably among these are Bernie Ragland of AT&T and Lex Roulston of Johnson &

Johnson, who have been a constant source of challenge to our ideas making sure that we avoid "going native" by thinking too traditionally. John Shank and Vijay Govindarajan of the Amos Tuck School at Dartmouth College and Tom Huff from the Wharton Executive Education program have listened to and challenged even our most out-landish theories.

Within Coopers & Lybrand there are far too many people to thank individually. The partners and the staff of the Information/Communications Industry practice pushed us to actually put pen to paper and acted as dedicated reviewers, especially Andy Zimmerman. The staff of the Financial Management and Business Analysis consulting practice were participants in many of the client engagements which shaped this book. Bob Janson has unsparingly lent us his expertise in how to change organizations and worked with our CFO clients as they struggle to affect transformational change. In addition, many others Coopers & Lybrand partners enthusiastically supported us and helped us introduce these concepts to their clients.

We cannot understate the value of Jon Zonderman in completing this effort. He listened to our musings and input and succeeded in pulling everything together into a coherent whole.

And finally, our thanks to all of our families, who have withstood not only the many long years of out of town assignments and late night report deadlines in service to our clients, but who also supported us throughout the ups and downs of getting this manuscript completed. Without their patience, support, and understanding none of this would have been possible.

To all of the above, we express our deepest gratitude.

Tom Walther
Hank Johansson
Jack Dunleavy
Beth Hjelm

Reinventing the CFO

1

A New Agenda for the Office of the CFO

Once upon a time all checks were green. All phones were black. Demand far outstripped supply and the United States owned the lion's share of the world's markets and productive capacity. Labor was expensive and materials cheap.

Management systems were designed to reflect this environment, with emphasis on mass production, throughput, labor productivity, and control. The financial systems and processes which were developed for the "modern" corporation worked beautifully and had a similar complexion.

- They were historical in nature.
- They were approval oriented.
- They were paper-based.
- They had centralized, compliance-based controls.

Since Western businesses began operating on these principles—around the 1920s—the world has changed dramatically. Most of that change has occurred in the last quarter of this century. The relative economic peace and tranquility that persisted through the 1960s has been shattered. Spiraling inflation and volatile interest rates began in the 1970s, as did the onset of true global competition. Since the late 1970s, there have been three economic recessions. Total government debt in the industrialized world has soared, cutting government flexibility in controlling economic activity through fiscal policy.

The pace of world economic change accelerated in the 1980s and early 1990s. Socialism collapsed. The United States economy has become increasingly deregulated, and Western European economies have moved to privatize former state-run services. There are new industrializing economies emerging from the ranks of the less-developed nations every year. Western multinationals have been buffeted by increasing globalization and the need to "think global and act local," to use the phrase of Percy Barnevik, chairman of the global engineering company Asea Brown Boveri. Over the same period, the electronic age has made operating truly global companies possible. Orders, payments, and capital move around the world at the speed of light through fiber-optic phone lines. Securities and currency trading are 24-hour operations.

Operating a large industrial, service, or financial services businesses is a nerve-racking way to go through life. The truth is simple, as James Brian Quinn argues in his book, *The Intelligent Enterprise:*

> If you can't focus and become the best in the world at what you do, making it very difficult for your competition to follow, your future cannot be insured!

Companies have tried to focus in a number of ways. They have engaged in balance sheet restructuring and planned downsizing. They have sought short-term solutions in cost-cutting efforts, much of which has focused on reducing people and bringing on board new technologies. At a deeper, more long-term level, they have engaged the philosophies of total quality management, with its ideas of problem solving and continuous improvement; just-in-time, which focuses on reducing cycle time and producing only what is necessary when it is needed; and more recently business process reengineering, which focuses on team-based process redesign and innovation.

All of these members of what we call the *process-oriented family* of management tools have as a strong focus the customer dimension, an external view. As companies have become more sophisticated in their use of these process-oriented tools, we believe a disconnect between operations and accounting is emerging. The reason is simple. While these philosophies have taken root on the operating side of businesses, the finance and accounting functions, which have traditionally been command-and-control oriented and internally focused, have remained largely in a functional silo. The transition to a process and knowledge-based orientation which has occurred in operations has been slower in finance. But now a new concept of the CFO is emerging around the globe.

Business process reengineering (BPR) categorizes accounting and finance as support processes, thereby relegating them to a position subservient to core processes. In the search for value-added processes to redesign or reengineer, BPR practitioners often find accounting and finance lacking—non-value adding—and ripe for outsourcing or elimination largely because they view accounting and finance as a bastion of paperwork and compliance. Unless CFOs and those who work for them accept the notion of value-added analysis, and redefine their roles around value-adding activities, they can look forward to more outsourcing, more elimination. Figure 1-1 shows how financial processes must be deeply integrated within the business's core processes, while others should be eliminated, redesigned, or moved into a shared-service model.

Until the mid-1980s, there had been no fundamental change in corporate finance and accounting since the 1920s and 30s. They were driven by principles of cost and management accounting developed in the 1920s as a way of imposing control on the operations designed through scientific management. And even the changes had been the first major changes in accounting principles since the invention of double-entry bookkeeping in 1497. The SEC Act of 1933 added rigor to accounting and forced accountants at public corporations to answer to two masters: the internal master of cost accounting and the external master of mandatory SEC reporting. The advent of mainframe computing in the 1960s added to corporate accounting headaches as much as it alleviated them. While computers certainly helped with record keeping, their ability to generate data by the pound led to increased number chasing. Management accounting, budgeting, planning, and responsibility accounting drove decision making yet they often resulted in counterproductive behavior. Complexity became fashionable.

Since the late 1980s, a quiet revolution has been building in corporate finance and accounting. More and more, companies are looking to their financial experts to act as business partners with operations managers and to dramatically reduce accounting and finance costs. However, changes in finance and accounting are still a generation behind operations management efforts that took root in the 1980s and running hard just to keep in place.

Sure, many CFOs are talking about changes that are required. But they need to do better in their actions; they need to bring their financial and accounting activities into line with the way they are operating their business. They need to help finance and accounting personnel adjust their roles and responsibilities to be value-adders, not merely number cops. And the way to do that is to reconstruct what is still often referred to as "the accounting function" into a true office of the chief financial officer. That's what this book is about. Over the last decade we have conducted a number of studies and worked with companies at the lead-

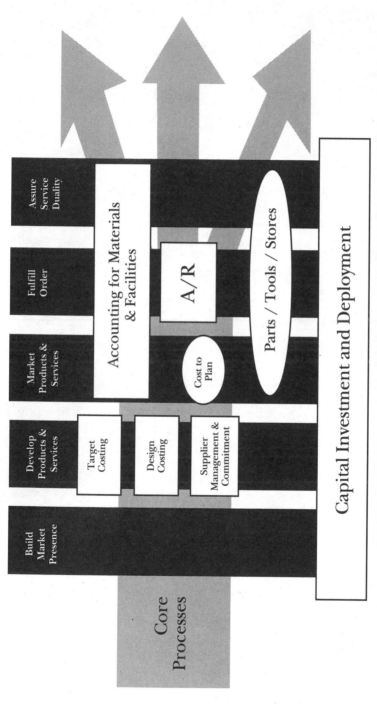

Figure 1-1. Financial processes are deeply embedded in core business processes; they are not stand-alone activities.

4

ing edge in transforming their financial operations. We have pieced together standards of excellence into a mosaic that we call the OCFO, the office of the chief financial officer.

Our experience with clients, benchmarking studies, the Financial Executives Research Foundation (FERF), academia, and our own Coopers & Lybrand CFO Forums indicate that:

- Expectations of the OCFO are high and ever increasing.
- The role of the CFO is changing dramatically.
- Business skills as well as traditional financial expertise are required not just by the CFO, but by all professionals within the OCFO.

While the CFO and those in the finance and accounting office were often thought of as number crunchers, budget drivers, data gatherers, and corporate cops, a new concept of the OCFO is developing based on expunging these old values and defining a new set of core competencies that define how the accounting and finance function performs, which include:

- Strong analytic focus on the business's drivers of success and operational strategies
- Controls achieved through process design
- Deep knowledge of the business
- Flexibility and a broad business perspective
- Clarity in communication

These core competencies relate to the OCFO's role as a provider of strategic analysis and appropriate measures, the source of *relevant* information and controls, and the keeper of effective and efficient processes and transaction systems. It's crucial to stress the importance of designing better processes and transaction systems than most corporations have today. A CFO who is slave to weak financial and operational systems and unintegrated processes will not have a controlled business. The CFO certainly will not have time to get out and do the important business of adding value to the company's operations.

A major study C&L conducted in 1989 showed that most CFOs were still spending 75 to 80 percent of their time on fiduciary issues, essentially outside reporting. Leading-edge CFOs were only spending about 25 to 30 percent of their time on fiduciary issues. But we believe the vision for the OCFO in the twenty-first century ought to be an office that spends only between 10 to 20 percent of its time on fiduciary issues. The rest of its time should be spent partnering with business operations executives in value-adding decision making for the business.

CFO magazine reported similarly gloomy results in 1993. It found that 66 percent of financial staff effort is spent on transactions, 18 percent on controls, 11 percent on decision support, and 5 percent on management. CFOs conclude from this that only about 20 percent of their office's effort is spent on value-adding activities.

CEOs can no longer look to increase the bottom line through cost cutting. They must now shift gears and look to grow the top line. Corporate finance and accounting can and should play an important role in meeting that goal. For the office of the CFO, the key is changing its image within the company: from negative to positive, from control that always says "no" to a partner that says "let's get it done." To do this the OCFO must stop being a victim of the transactions it processes and enrich the job content of its personnel by relegating decision making to the personnel that have the most direct contact with customers. The issue is "how?"

Figure 1-2 shows how the work of the OCFO overlaps the work of three other key business areas—the CEO and the executive team, operations, and marketing. Aligning the work of the OCFO to the work of these other corporate players is the key to partnering and adding value. There are many boundary areas where finance must interact effectively with other key business partners to provide value to the company. None of these areas is the exclusive domain of one discipline. Partnering is accomplished most successfully if it is approached as a team effort.

The CFO's New Agenda

The new agenda has five components, each of which is discussed in its own chapter. In our final chapter, we discuss the organizational issues that need to be dealt with in changing the OCFO itself. The five components are:

1. Partnering and integrating finance into the business
2. Strategy
3. Management control
4. Cost management
5. Processes and systems

Thinking of the OCFO's role in this way is totally new. Figure 1-3 shows a more traditional way of looking at the OCFO's role. This might be called the OCFO house. Within this house reside all of the activities, tasks, and responsibilities found in a traditional office of the CFO. There is an implied hierarchy. Unfortunately, this hierarchy is incompatible

Figure 1-2. Being a partner means aligning finance with other players.

with modern realities. You might want to refer back to this graphic as you read on, noticing how we take seemingly disparate elements and weave them into what we believe are more logical groupings.

Partnering and Integration

There is no predetermined template for organizational integration. However, there are some common questions that must be asked and answered.

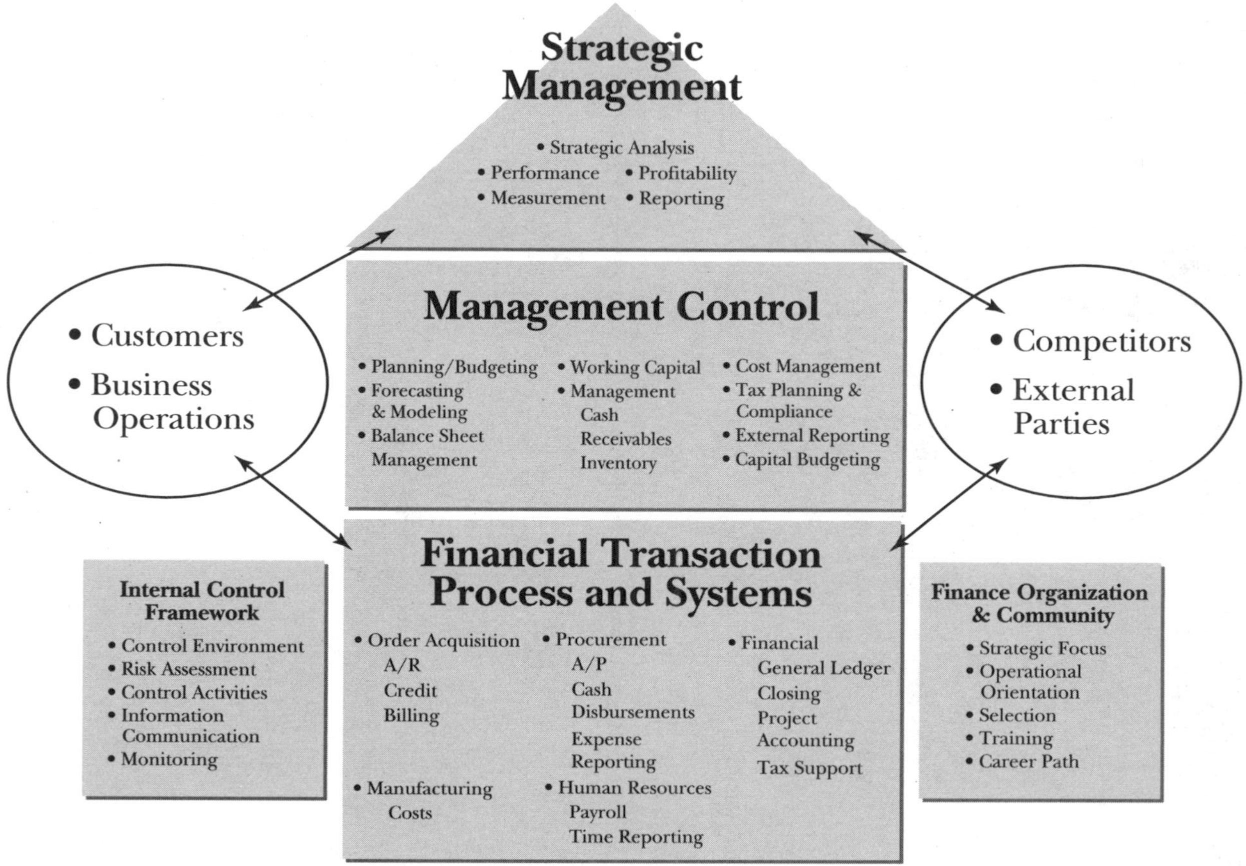

Figure 1-3. The "house" of the OCFO.

What are the roles and responsibilities of the OCFO? It used to be a bookkeeper, numbers cop. Now it is a partner in such areas as performance reporting, pricing, and product development.

How will the OCFO be structured? The OCFO still needs to be a resource for the finance community, shareholders, and the SEC. But internally, it needs to work more closely with other areas of the business.

Who are the people who populate the OCFO? Where do they come from? How are they trained and how should the company train them? This is perhaps the largest challenge for the OCFO. No longer can the office recruit and attract people with the old accounting mindset, people who are seen as transaction processors, and who all too often are seen as costs rather than assets. The OCFO must recruit and retain bright, creative people who define their responsibilities in terms of strategic and analytic collaboration across departmental lines.

We'll discuss selection, training, and development of the right kinds of people for this new role, and how to work to change the culture of the financial community within your own business. We'll also discuss career paths and reward systems for OCFO personnel.

Strategy

In the strategy arena, the OCFO needs to provide the strategic analysis and insights which ensure operations managers take intelligent risks and reach consistent decisions. One key tool is value-chain analysis that looks at both the company's internal value chain and the company's position in the industry value chain.

The OCFO must develop a close relationship with marketing teams to help analyze the company's value to customers by adding quantitative rigor to such marketing questions as: What customers do we value the most? What do those customers value about our product and service? What is the cost of service, and what is the cost of adding more value for the customer? This external value perception will drive the internal value chain. Through this value-chain analysis, both external and internal, the OCFO has a key role to play in analyzing strategic investments, framing competitor analysis, evaluating core business processes, and linking strategy to implementation.

It's no longer enough to produce historic product and customer profitability analyses; in today's fiercely competitive environment analysis of profit opportunity is also necessary. With clear, strong analysis from the OCFO companies can achieve more *breakpoints*—changes in product, quality, or service that lead to a significant increase in market share.

Management Control

It's no longer enough to be the corporate cop. Today's OCFO must deliver balanced measures and value-added analysis in real time. Traditional measures are too numerous, too internal, and too "dollarized." New measures need to be designed to answer such questions as Where is the business going? How are we doing on that journey? and What is the long-term, least-cost structure to get there?

Measures need to tie actions to corporate strategy and look more to the value chain and not merely the balance sheet. The bottom line is that, increasingly, financial management is not what drives companies' results. What drives results is how products and services deliver value to customers.

Cost Management

Historically, cost accounting systems were designed with Taylor's scientific management theory in mind. Consequently, they focused heavily on labor content and productivity. In many cases they provided the wrong answers about product cost that resulted in counterproductive behavior, such as building up inventory to absorb overhead.

Leading CFOs understand that the key to the cost side is not cost accounting, or even cost cutting. It is cost management. They implement cost management systems that are forward focused, provide relevant cost information, and create an environment for cost control and even cost reduction.

Systems and Processes

The key to all of this is optimizing the effectiveness and efficiency of managing the financial processes and supporting the core business processes.

Core business processes are those activities that are critical to running the business. By definition financial processes are not core but rather supporting processes. However, some financial processes are key to the effective functioning of the core business. It is important that financial personnel understand the end-to-end nature of core business processes and the drivers of performance.

One goal of the financial community must be to develop the appropriate performance measures, or key performance indicators (KPIs), both financial and operational. These should be linked to the company's strategies and focus on measures such as customer service, market penetration, human resources, productivity, cycle time, and quality, as well as cost. The OCFO must be able to provide timely support information and analysis using these measures. The result is value-added and integrated support of the business.

Key financial processes need to be deeply integrated into the company's core business processes. Those financial processes that are closely linked to the core business processes can be leveraged or redesigned so they can be leveraged. Transaction-based processes that are not closely aligned are candidates for service sharing, outsourcing, or even elimination, as they would be in a factory focused on efficiency and productivity.

Three central questions must be asked in evaluating financial processes:

1. Is the process an asset or a liability?
2. How important is the process?
3. How can the process be optimized?

Process changes can be made to optimize routine processes and make them competitive assets of the business not simply infrastructure. For instance, MCI took a background process that was a liability, a non-value-adding process—billing—and turned it into a competitive advantage by creating "Friends and Family," which became a key marketing tool in the early 1980s.

How to Use This Book

Although it is possible to read this book by going directly to the chapters that most concern you, we would suggest reading Chapter 2, on the issue of business partnership, before getting into the chapters that detail the various aspects of that partnership.

Each chapter contains what we call *QuickGrids* and *Difficulty Maps*. The QuickGrid is a way for you to map where your company is along the continuum from lagging to leading in any particular set of OCFO competencies. The difficulty charts have two parts. The top half of the chart plots a curve of where we believe the universe of CFO organizations falls, given our studies and work with major clients. The bottom half shows the degree of difficulty of moving from the left or "lagging" side of the scale to the right or "leading" side. Both the distribution of companies and the difficulty are different for each of the elements in the CFOs new agenda.

There are four appendixes in the book. Appendixes A and B are each aligned with both Chapters 2 and 7. Appendix A contains questions to ask your "internal customers" regarding the as-is state of your OCFO. This is a necessary early step in creating a vision for the new OCFO and should be reviewed while undergoing the implementation of that vision. Appendix B is a survey for the OCFO staff that helps those leading the change effort understand the OCFO organization's readiness and willingness to change, how well the OCFO is doing along a number of dimensions, and what priorities people would assign to various change issues.

While much of this book exhorts CFOs to move beyond their traditional command and control role, many of our clients still face the enormous task of rationalizing and simplifying their transaction processes. Appendixes C and D both relate to the issues around transaction systems and processes discussed in Chapter 6. Appendix C is a benchmarking template that shows how to collect data on some of the traditional financial processes and what some of the data elements are that you will need to focus on. Appendix D shows an abstract of some benchmark data developed by using the data elements discussed in Appendix C.

2

Business Partnership

Business partnership forms the backbone of any reinvention of the finance community. It is not enough to say "I want this to be a world-class Office of the CFO." It is not enough to say "I want the Office of the CFO to add value" or "...to become a business partner."

At a minimum, organizational integration and business partnership requires that the OCFO define its roles, responsibilities, goals, and objectives. With that as a starting point, the organization must answer the following question: How does the financial organization find and develop the right people with the right balance of financial, operational, and entrepreneurial capabilities? It requires a top-to-bottom analysis of the skills, structure, processes, technology, and culture of the company's financial community. This involves looking at not only the people within the organization, but also the CFO's own leadership skills and what personnel and policies can be developed to complement those leadership skills. It is important to remember that against this backdrop, the OCFO is being asked to do more with less.

To put it simply, it is a different world view from that traditionally thought of as the finance view—it requires that people look forward rather than back and that people seek long-term stability rather than simply short-term profit.

Many CFOs claim they are business partners, citing as evidence their attendance at monthly financial evaluations and their role as the driver of the budget process, yet few truly achieve partnership status. While a rare few have reached the point of contributing to value creation on a number of different levels, most remain in their historical role of score keeping and maintain their command-and-control posture.

Those OCFOs that have really become partners have struck the appropriate balance between *effectiveness* in value creation and *efficiency* in their control role.

A Command-Control Tradition

The traditional command-and-control orientation of the financial organization has deep historical origins. Much of the typical OCFO finds its roots in Frederick Taylor's scientific theory of management. This theory is efficiency-oriented, breaking down work into ever more discreet, simple, and repetitive tasks that can be performed by less skilled employees. In the financial office, this turns the professional role of fiscal resource management into a semiskilled clerical job.

Scientific management is also driven by micromanagement and universally imposed discipline. The discipline is ladened with voluminous, complex, and detailed rules that are not easily understood or interpreted by the rest of the business community. The keepers of these rules and imposers of financial management discipline include the Financial Accounting Standards Board (FASB), the Internal Revenue Service and state and local taxing authorities, and the numerous federal, state, and local regulatory agencies.

In addition, in publicly held corporations, the OCFO has a fiduciary responsibility to individual stockholders and marketplace "players," including money managers, pension fund executives, analysts and others. This fiduciary role has often led to a negative view of the OCFO. Those who work within the financial organization are seen, and often see themselves, as bean counters who wear green eye shades, and are overly nitpicky and detailed in their focus on meeting external compliance needs, preventing cheating and stealing and in their constant search for what's wrong (i.e., budget variances). .

This historical role has encased the OCFO in a functional silo. Although, from the early 1980s on, many companies have sought to move from functional definitions of work to cross-functional value-creating teams and processes, there has been little effort to break down the barriers around the OCFO function.

This is due partly to a mindset that has developed within the OCFO, where people who think of their fiduciary and fiscal cop roles as primary have been hired and trained. As a result, the rest of the organization does not want to bring the OCFO into the value-creating team and process model for fear that the OCFO will seek to impose its traditional rules and measures on this new way of working. CFOs who want to move successfully into the twenty-first century must strike an appropriate balance between their traditional fiduciary role and the need to create value for the organization.

The New Fiduciary View

CFOs and their organizations can in no way abandon their fiduciary responsibility. But this role cannot be looked upon as the organization's sole role. The CFO must take a fresh look at how the financial organization approaches its fiduciary obligations.

- Policies and procedures need to be revisited in terms of practicality and relevance and revised as necessary.
- Controls should be built into processes as enablers and not imposed externally to the process as barriers.
- Cost and cycle time should be given high priority when building the fiduciary control environment.

Value Creation: The New Role

Value creation is a new role for the OCFO in many companies. This new responsibility, which brings the finance organization to the table as a true business partner, can be addressed by offering the following:

1. *Insightful contributions into the strategy and planning process.* The finance organization can be indispensable in assisting the company define and focus on its core competencies. It is also in the best position to perform value-chain analysis. And it can be increasingly helpful in competitive investigations and analyses.

2. *Measures that focus and motivate the organization.* The finance organization needs to work with executive and operations management in the creation of measures that have a strategic focus, are balance between financial and operational, and are predictive rather than retrospective.

3. *Information and analysis that provides insight into how value is being created and how progress is being matched to strategic initiatives.* The information provided from the financial organization to executive management must have a future direction and lead to corrective action.

4. *Leadership of major financial initiatives.* The financial organization is in a unique position to provide leadership in creating long-term cost management and capital utilization decisions.

Effectiveness or Efficiency?

Our experience with clients shows that the office of the CFO in the 1990s and beyond can truly add value by focusing on some of the value-creating themes discussed above. However, if the CFO focuses purely on fiduciary tasks, controls, transaction processing, and infrastructure support, the OCFO will be efficiency driven. If the CFO chooses to concentrate instead on value creation, then there will be an effectiveness-driven organizational transformation.

Figure 2-1 shows some of the methods of driving the transformation in an efficiency direction. Figure 2-2 shows some of the methods of driving the transformation in an effectiveness direction.

Efficiency

Most organizations begin the transformation of their financial function by taking the efficiency route. It is tangible and often produces significant cost savings and other benefits.

Striving for efficiency is often the easier route, although it can involve costly process and system redesigns for necessary but non-value-added work. Organizations can be delayered and spans of control increased.

There is increasing acceptance of outsourcing and shared services

Efficiency Drivers

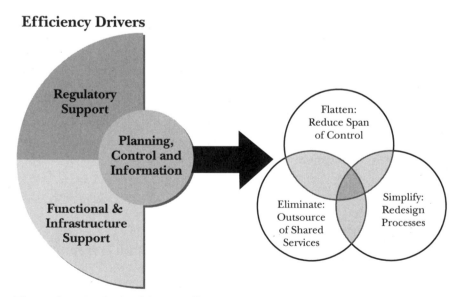

Figure 2-1. Methods of driving efficiency in the OCFO.

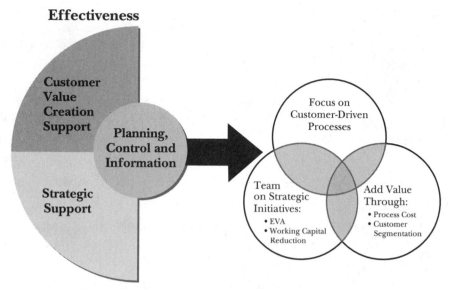

Figure 2-2. Methods of driving effectiveness in the OCFO.

alternatives for processes that are not considered strategic (i.e., tax compliance or transaction processing centers). A number of excellent vendors provide these services and a growing number of corporations with multiple business units are moving toward central financial transaction shared services at the same time they're allowing more decentralization of strategic business unit (SBU) management decisions.

CFOs can turn to one of a host of books on process redesign for a head start on what tactics should be considered. Similarly, any one of a number of centers that offer benchmarking assistance can provide metrics for cost comparison and get people into a network, making it easier to share ideas. A couple of noteworthy examples are the Continuous Improvement Center of the Institute of Management Accountants and the Benchmarking program of the American Institute of Certified Public Accountants.

Effectiveness

We have found that it is a lot harder to work on effectiveness. It is difficult to readily incorporate lessons from other companies, since the relative importance of the OCFO working on customer-driven processes or strategic initiatives is really dependent upon the executive level of support and the skills and competencies of the OCFO itself. The bulk of this book is, in fact, focused on how the OCFO can address questions of adding value through planning, measurement, analytical information, and leadership of financial initiatives.

Beginning the Transformation

Before companies embark on major changes in the office of the CFO, we believe they would do well to ask themselves three fundamental questions:

1. What is the CFO organization's primary role now, and what should it be in the future?
2. How can the CFO become a business partner?
3. Is the CFO organization involved and knowledgeable about the business?

It is important to ask these questions at the outset to help gauge the degree of change management external to the finance organization that will be necessary—in other words, how much of an attitude change will be necessary in the rest of the company about the role of the CFO and the finance team.

Figure 2-3 shows how a number of finance managers and general managers from some of our clients answered these questions. These results closely mirror results *CFO* magazine received to similar questions in 1993.

There are a number of important lessons to be drawn from Figure 2-3. First, as should have been expected, operations counterparts—finance organization customers—have a different perception than the finance organization itself, as shown by the gaps in the answers.

The second lesson, and to us an even more striking one, is that within the finance organization itself, only 30 percent of personnel believe they are truly a business partner and less than two-thirds believe they are involved in and knowledgeable about the business. Clearly, most organizations have a need for both external and internal change management.

The next step is for the CFO to do some soul searching as to where his or her organization stands. Clearly, in the best of all worlds every CFO organization would be driven by the effectiveness issues while ensuring an acceptable level of efficiency. Our QuickGrid shows where we think leading-edge CFO organizations ought to be moving. By using the

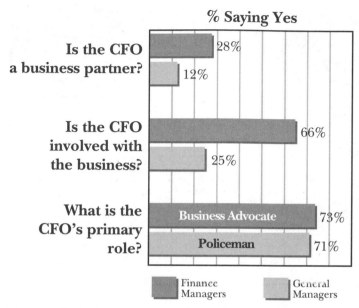

Figure 2-3. Differing perceptions of finance.

LAGGING	BEHIND	MEDIAN	AHEAD	LEADING
CONFORMER	**REACTOR**	**CONTROLLER**	**TEAM PLAYER**	**TEAM LEADER**
• Basic finance	• Occasional	• Financial	• Integrated	• Teamworker
• Separate	analysis	control of	functions	• Shared values
functions	• Reluctant	operations	• Cross function	• Value creator
• Focus on control	participator	• Traditional	training	• Delivers results
& compliance	• Occasional	oversight	• Shared goals	• Manages
• Regulations	member	• Role	• Accepts project	competencies
• Bureaucratic	of teams	reinforcer	responsibility	and skills
	• Aloof	• Organizational	• Manages	• Market focus
		hierachy	strengths	• Sought out
				for business
				knowledge

Figure 2-4. Comparative positioning on C&L's QuickGrid—business partnership.

QuickGrid shown in Figure 2-4, you should be able to determine where your finance organization is currently and create a goal for how quickly you think you should be moving toward the right on the grid.

As you look at the QuickGrid, it's important to keep in mind Figure 2-5, the top half of which plots the distribution curve and the bottom half of which shows the difficulty of moving to the right on the QuickGrid. It is

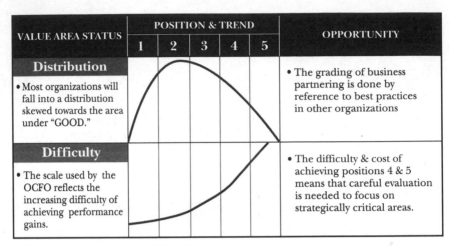

VALUE AREA STATUS	POSITION & TREND					OPPORTUNITY
	1	2	3	4	5	
Distribution • Most organizations will fall into a distribution skewed towards the area under "GOOD."						• The grading of business partnering is done by reference to best practices in other organizations
Difficulty • The scale used by the OCFO reflects the increasing difficulty of achieving performance gains.						• The difficulty & cost of achieving positions 4 & 5 means that careful evaluation is needed to focus on strategically critical areas.

Figure 2-5. Comparative difficulty chart—business partnership.

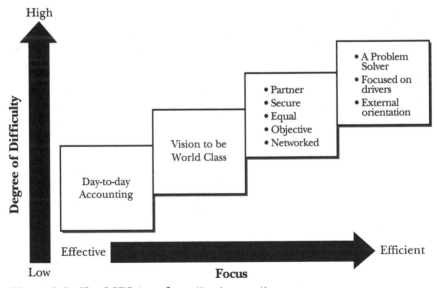

Figure 2-6. The OCFO transformation is a continuum.

also important to understand that the transformation is a continuum of building blocks, as shown in Figure 2-6.

After the basic day-to-day accounting transaction and control processes are in place, a vision for becoming world class can be created. The CFO and CEO need to agree to this vision for the OCFO, and both must share that vision with the financial organization.

Through this vision, the CFO begins to become a true partner in the business, equal in contribution as well as position with other executives, and actively involved in business decisions. Yet the CFO remains objective and still leads the rest of the executive team to execute their fiduciary responsibilities.

Partnering is mature when the OCFO becomes a truly value-creating entity. This comes about when the financial organization continuously improves its processes, leverages deep operational knowledge, and is externally focused on operational problem solving and strategic drivers.

Creating and Developing the Vision

Remember, moving along and up the continuum involves major change: developing new skills, adopting new structures or changing old ones, engineering or reengineering processes, embracing new technology, and changing the finance culture. To effect this change, the CFO must articulate a firm vision that defines a compelling need to change and communicates that need to the entire financial organization.

We have seen many OCFO vision statements full of the right words (business partner, customer orientation, commitment to quality, etc.). Yet often these organizations lack the real internalized conviction about how work will be done and how the OCFO will change and grow intellectually. And, moreover, they lack an action plan that will achieve the change needed.

Developing a vision can only be done by a small team, representing all levels of the OCFO organization. That team should probably go through at least a brief team training exercise, including some problem-solving, and then should be given a little information about the technical aspects of the entire OCFO function.

The vision has to be developed in the context of the company's relationship to its industry and any special circumstances the company or the industry face. The vision must outline the organizational culture that *should be* in place in order for the vision to be possible. And, finally, the vision must clearly signal what behaviors are expected and what priorities have been established to guide the OCFO as it reinvents itself.

Sometimes the CFO can encounter a cultural roadblock, and the vision of the OCFO, which is running out ahead of the curve, must be tempered in order to align with the rest of leadership. Other times, the CFO's vision for his or her office is not keeping pace with the corporate vision and must be pulled into alignment with the larger corporate vision.

For example, a roadblock situation might look like the following. We were once called in by the corporate controller of a $5 billion high-tech equipment manufacturing and service company who wanted to reorient the finance organization to work more closely with operations. The controller had read lots of articles and studied many of the well-known case studies of leading finance organizations. She had become convinced that embarking on a similar change at her company would add real value to the business and make the finance organization a more attractive place to work within the company.

This all sounded terrific. But there was a problem. The company had emerged from a significant reorganization a few years earlier, and the current CEO had been the CFO during that time. He was cut from the traditional command-and-control cloth. There was a lot of uncertainty in the market about the company's long-term viability, and the company was still heavily focused on cash flow. The CFO had also been actively involved in the company's reorganization and had some dynamic ideas.

The CEO had put together a new management team, with experts who had come from other companies heading up different market segments. He had one person to whom he looked for strategic planning and advice and another to whom he looked for operational performance information. All of the different segment heads worked to eliminate non-value-adding activities and manage the long-term cost structure through business process reengineering while looking for new products to create a long-term revenue stream.

What the CEO wanted from the CFO was that the books be kept in good order and that capital expenditures be controlled with an iron fist. He wanted the CFO to be a highly cost-efficient processor of financial transactions who oversaw a well-controlled global environment.

But the controller had a staff of extremely bright people who truly understood the business and its cost structure. In most cases they were highly regarded by their business partners in operations and valued for their analytic expertise. In addition, the OCFO had made some notable progress in the United States in developing a data warehousing capability and integrating financial and nonfinancial information for business case analyses.

Despite this, budgeting, planning, and management reporting were done just like the textbooks—lots of detail, numbers cut in every way possible, the illusion of bottoms-up while the final target was really determined by the top overall targets required. Budgeting and reporting were used as control tools, not as value-added tools for the business. Moreover, the level of detail really reflected the crisis mentality that had been in place for several years.

The CFO saw the need to dramatically simplify these processes and reduce the timetable dramatically for both budget preparation and the monthly and quarterly management reports. She also wanted to change the focus of the processes to be predictive rather than retrospective. In these aims, she was supported by much of the senior executive team.

Of the two areas where she focused her effort to change processes, the most dramatic and immediate benefit was in the area of the monthly and quarterly performance review meetings. First, she changed the level of detail that was reported during those meetings. Predictive key indicators of business performance became the focus for the reports. Financial results were no longer the majority of the information reported. Trends and industry issues were a primary topic for discussion, along with the implications for the projected results over the next quarter and the next year. The presumption was made that the detail still existed in the company's operational and accounting systems, although it was no longer printed out in 2-inch thick reports.

Even more importantly, the CFO managed to get the format for the sessions changed. Instead of a 3-day meeting, where the head of each business came in with an entourage of support analysts and formally presented results to the executive team, SBU executives came in by themselves.

Instead of a retrospectively focused meeting, with senior executives pressing for extreme levels of detail—which some likened to an inquisition—each SBU head gave a brief overview of key performance indicators, financial information, and market trends; details were asked for only in the exceptional instance. Meetings were scaled back to 1 day, and there was still time for senior executives to discuss cross-SBU issues.

Although he was reluctant to go to this format, fearing that things would fall through the cracks, the CEO agreed to a trial period. During that period, the OCFO worked diligently with him, assuring him that the group was still in command of the detail but getting him to focus more on operational and predictive issues rather than on financial and retrospective aspects of performance.

If the previous example shows how organizational culture blocked the finance organization from moving forward as fast as the CFO would like, other companies provide examples of senior management requiring the CFO and the finance organization to stretch much further than it naturally would.

One such example is provided by one of the largest credit card companies in the United States. From its start-up, the company has prided itself on moving quickly in a very competitive industry and providing its customers with superb service.

Because of the competitive nature of the credit card industry, the senior executive team understood that the company needed to become as sophisticated as rapidly as possible in the identification of successful marketing themes and campaigns, as well as in the analysis of customer profitability over the life cycle of their relationship with the company. Banks were increasingly introducing their own competing credit cards, and companies like Shell Oil, General Motors, Ford, and even Toys R Us were introducing their own co-branded credit cards.

In response, the company understood that it needed to hone its overall capital allocation and investment analysis processes and to begin the process of managing its long-term capital structure through the elimination of non-value-added activities. In these efforts, the OCFO was expected to take a leadership role.

To systematize and improve the analysis of customer segment profitability, as well as marketing campaign effectiveness, the company undertook a project designed to develop sophisticated costing and segmentation analysis. The result was an important analysis tool for the company to look at its overall effectiveness in the market and compare the success rates over multiple periods of various marketing campaigns and segmentation approaches. Finance's primary role was to define the business rules to support an analytic framework, and to create a model that reflected the business environment.

Articulating the Vision

Vision statements cannot be overly broad. They must give those to whom they are presented a clear idea of not only the direction the financial organization is going, but the relative importance of the various areas of excellence sought.

As we said earlier, the CFO must articulate a firm vision that both defines the compelling need to change and communicates that need to the entire financial organization. The vision must also be shared with all of the other areas of the business with which the OCFO will work in partnership. The vision statement must guide the organization and provide the "glue" that holds the organization together while it develops and internalizes its conviction to change and grow.

Much has been written about vision statements. Almost every organization today has one. While we could have easily picked a vision statement from any number of companies, there are two we think amplify the themes discussed in this chapter and throughout the rest of the book—the vision statements of the finance organizations at Johnson & Johnson and AT&T.

The current Johnson & Johnson vision statement, excerpted below, is an excellent example of what finance organizations should strive for.

This statement is not the first the company developed—the J&J finance group has been working for years on reducing the overall non-value-added activities it performs, increasing its strategic partnership with the company's operational areas, and defining those few key areas where finance can—and must—lead the business. We have picked this vision statement as an example because it:

- Focuses on the select areas where the organization has a demonstrable competence and can add value to the business
- Addresses the "what" and the "how" and ties the key initiatives together with overall goals
- Integrates the organization's required behavior with the attitudes and values that must drive that behavior
- Clearly defines measures of performance against which the organization's success will be evaluated—reduced cycle time, work simplification, and reduced costs
- Reflects the need to continually renew the people in the organization and helps them develop intellectually so they are personally challenged

In its finance vision statement Johnson & Johnson lists five areas in which it will excel:

1. Business partnership
2. Organizational excellence
3. Technological leadership
4. Cash and tax management
5. Audit and control

Under business partnership, J&J states that its basic objective is to:

Act as a business partner and to be productive and innovative in the application of financial knowledge and techniques to help solve business problems and maximize business opportunities.

For organizational excellence, the company states that its basic objective is to:

Achieve organizational excellence by developing and maintaining a strong organization with self-perpetuating characteristics and high standards in a creative and productive atmosphere.

For technological leadership, the basic objective is to:

Maintain technological leadership by ensuring optimal efficiency in our systems and computer operations and build strategic business alliances with our customers and suppliers. Capitalize on advancements in information technology.

For cash and tax management, the basic objective is to:

Take a leadership role in the conservation of assets, control of spending, management of taxes and management of cash flow.

In the area of audit and control, the basic objective is to:

Maintain an internal control environment which will provide management with reasonable assurances that assets are safeguarded from unauthorized use or disposition and that financial records are accurate and reliable. To ensure that the requirements are met in an effective and efficient manner and are flexible enough to adapt to changing business conditions or requirements. Due consideration should be given to appropriate automation applications and resource limitations.

Notice the order in which the five areas are addressed—from the macro and companywide, business partnering, to the micro and finance-specific, cash and tax, and audit and control.

Another notable example of a vision statement is that of AT&T. With just a few words, the vision defines the financial community's aspirations: "One CFO Team: Best and Fastest—Together." The vision statement was laid out in terms of achieving goals in:

1. Business processes, services, and controls

2. Business analysis

3. Business partnering

Unlike the J&J vision statement, the AT&T statement is global rather than focused. It is an excellent example of how a vision statement can be used to mobilize an organization and communicate the need and direction of the change required.

We need to give you a little background. The AT&T finance organization in 1995 numbered about 18,000 employees at the corporate level and within its many businesses and groups across the world. The pace of competition in the information and telecommunications industry had heightened and accelerated to the point that it was absolutely critical that the long-term cost structure of business be reduced across all of the company's processes.

Moreover, the finance organization at the time was being asked to do a lot more with a lot less—to add value through analysis, to rethink the way the business is structured, and to provide better and faster information. While the finance organization was being challenged in these areas, an even greater challenge was to develop a really strong sense of community within the organization, to get finance to work together across the historically strong and powerful divisional and group boundaries.

We chose this vision statement because it:

- Clearly articulates how the major forces affecting the competitiveness of the business overall also require a change in finance.

- Is honest. The vision statement explains that the finance organization is not world class in many areas that are important as the business goes forward, despite the years of priding itself as one of the world's largest corporations. Size does not always mean best in class, and tackling that issue head on is important if real change is to be accomplished.

- Integrates the required organizational behavior with the attitudes and values that must drive the behavior—the rallying cry of "Best, Fastest, Together," combined with the five elements of "the common bond"—respect, integrity, teamwork, dedication, and innovation.

- Articulates what finance is really supposed to do, not just controls and transactions services but business analysis and business partnering.

- Begins to address the "what" and the "how" by tying together the key initiatives with the overall goals.

- Includes some answers to questions that individuals throughout the organization were asking about goals, how things were going to be different, and what was really meant by the CFO community.

Getting the Organization into Line

Vision includes a definition of what those processes are, what the process capabilities are, and what competencies are necessary to create or enhance process capabilities. Process capabilities include quality, cycle time, and cost and service metrics directly linked to financial customers and to running the business.

As we stated in our book, *Best Practices in Reengineering*, "to control and shape the direction of change, a company must develop a thorough understanding of the desired state—what executives want the company to be like in three to five years—and of the current state....The size of the gap between the desired and current states argues for the compelling need to change. In short, the pain of remaining in the current state has to be worse than the pain involved in trying to make change occur."

In theory, once a leader of a company, or in this instance the OCFO, has defined the compelling need for change, people throughout the organization should be willing to make the change. But in reality, causing change is much more difficult. Leaders must gauge their organization's readiness to change before attempting the reengineering effort, which is perhaps the largest organizational change effort a company, division, or internal organization such as the OCFO will ever undergo.

As most of us know, financial organizations are notoriously change averse since change involves risk, and finance personnel are trained to be risk averse. It is therefore critical to evaluate the OCFO organization in both its human resources dimensions and its structure.

After the vision is defined, the compelling need to change identified and articulated, and the level of readiness to change judged, the organization must commit resources—people and capital—to affecting the change. Taking a cue from successful process reengineers, this should be accomplished by undertaking one or two major initiatives at a time. We'll discuss the mechanics of implementing the vision in our final chapter.

At this point, however, it is important to realize that an understanding of where the financial organization should be in the desired state requires mapping of the current financial organization's processes at a high level. This mapping provides a performance baseline and gives the financial office members an understanding of problems, their root causes, and the need to depart from the as-is situation.

One issue we have seen in every company that we have worked with in an effort to create world-class CFO organizations is the struggle over what kind of human capital is required in this new environment. It is clear that in effectiveness-driven OCFOs, there is a need for skills that many current employees don't have. Also, as shown earlier, whether the primary drivers are effectiveness or efficiency, the world-class OCFO is 30 to 50 percent leaner than most current finance organizations.

Skills Are Not Competencies

Financial expertise needs to be augmented with additional skills. Finance staff need to be able to work effectively with teams. To do this, they need not only interpersonal and communication skills, but an enterprise perspective, initiative, and organizational savvy. In many instances they will need to work across national boundaries, possibly in many languages.

CFOs need to ask five questions at the outset:

1. What skills and competencies are required?
2. What skills and competencies does my organization have?
3. How should I select who stays?
4. Where should I look to find the new talent that I require, and what training do these people need about my unique business character- istics and processes?
5. What should I do about training and developing those who remain?

Figure 2-7 shows some of the economic and market challenges facing many of today's industries along with the corresponding shift in skills needed within the office of the CFO.

Individuals who enter the value-oriented office of the CFO will need specific technical and personal skills and industry expertise.

Among technical skills are such traditional skills as general account- ing, transactions management, treasury and cash management, and statutory corporate reporting. But the new toolbox of technical skills also includes business process redesign and reengineering, activity- based cost management, and the use of breakthrough performance measures.

At the industry level, individuals will need to know industry dynam- ics and drivers, comparative and competitive analysis, and the industry's value chain today and tomorrow.

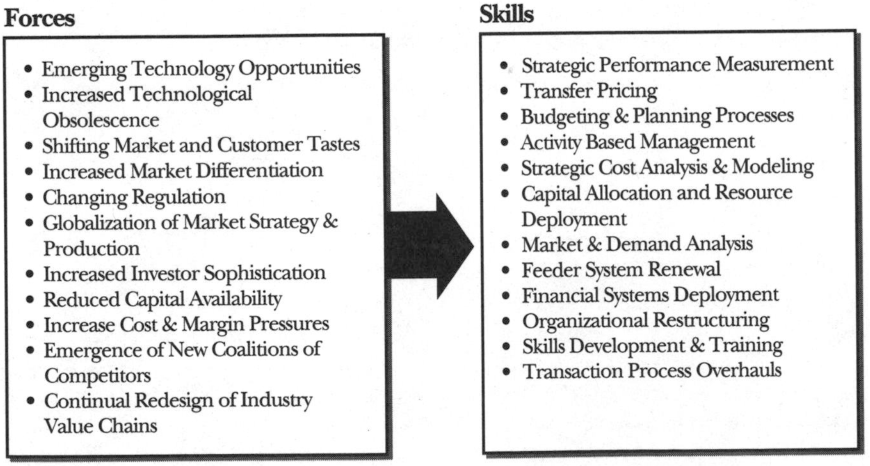

Forces

- Emerging Technology Opportunities
- Increased Technological Obsolescence
- Shifting Market and Customer Tastes
- Increased Market Differentiation
- Changing Regulation
- Globalization of Market Strategy & Production
- Increased Investor Sophistication
- Reduced Capital Availability
- Increase Cost & Margin Pressures
- Emergence of New Coalitions of Competitors
- Continual Redesign of Industry Value Chains

Skills

- Strategic Performance Measurement
- Transfer Pricing
- Budgeting & Planning Processes
- Activity Based Management
- Strategic Cost Analysis & Modeling
- Capital Allocation and Resource Deployment
- Market & Demand Analysis
- Feeder System Renewal
- Financial Systems Deployment
- Organizational Restructuring
- Skills Development & Training
- Transaction Process Overhauls

Figure 2-7. Shifting skills requirements in the office of the CFO.

Personal skills include facilitation and team building, leadership and change management skills, and strategic thinking.

It's important to remember that skills are not competencies. Competencies are a collection of integrated intellectual assets, a sum, rather than a single technical capability. As Gary Hamel and C. K. Prahalad discuss in *Competing for the Future*, "the starting premise is that competition between firms is as much a race for competence mastery as it is for market position and market power." Competencies which are truly "core" must:

- Contribute to customer value
- Differentiate the company from its competitors
- Form the basis for future market or product activities

The reason why the notion of competencies is important to the OCFO is that finance's own collection of assets must complement and be driven by the competencies of the business overall. In order to reinvent the OCFO people should not be looked at in terms of their technical or functional skills, but instead in terms of their "fit" with the overall organizational competencies.

We believe competencies for individuals within the OCFO can be thought of in three groups:

1. Personal Effectiveness, which includes a bias for action, an orientation that accepts and embraces change, leadership qualities, and a learning and knowledge orientation.
2. Shared Effectiveness, which includes effectiveness in teams, effectiveness in an environment that "empowers" and grants autonomy, and a set of values that embraces diversity.
3. Process Effectiveness, which includes relationship building and process-oriented thinking.

Each of these can be deconstructed even further as shown in Figure 2-8.

Finding people with the right skills and competencies is no easy task. Although some people who have been in the corporate OCFO environment for long periods of time have these skills and competencies, many others do not. Determining who can function in the new way of working and who can't is itself a difficult task. Then there is the issue of how much and what kind of training is necessary to sharpen and build the skills and competencies that have most likely lain dormant even in those who have them.

Turning to business schools for the next generation of OCFO personnel is equally problematic, since many business school curriculums are,

Finance Organization Competency Assessment–Systems Thinking

Definition–Systems Thinking:
- Understanding the work of the organization within the broader context of an integrated system and linking the results of that work with the purpose of the system and the achievement of a shared vision and set of goals.

Behaviors:

Understands Finance's contribution and impact:
- Effectively organizes work by breaking down tasks and activities in a logical manner
- Cooperates with others to set priorities for actions that fit within Finance's goals
- Actively works to improve quality by understanding the linkage between units

Understands process contributions/impacts:
- Analyzes relationships among multiple parts of a problem or within a process
- Understands the impact of changes on the broader process
- Generally anticipates process obstacles and thinks ahead about next steps
- Sets work unit goals that fit into process goals and continuously drives to understand and improve process performance

Understands enterprisewide contributions/impacts:
- Sets process performance goals that fit with the overall aim or vision of the organization performance
- Understands the structure and working of the organization and makes decisions that promote improvements in the overall performance of the organization

Understands industry and market impacts:
- Understands the broader market and industry forces and how they impact enterprise-level decision
- Is able to manage the impacts of changes in markets and industry forces by analyzing the implications for the enterprise, evaluating strategic options and prioritizing enterprise-level changes necessary to ensure the continued success of the organization
- Is able to modify, when necessary, objectives, strategies and tactics used to accomplish organizational goals

Figure 2-8. Assess competencies, not skills.

if anything, behind the industrial curve in this area, continuing to focus on discreet skills rather than overarching competencies in such areas as analysis, team work, and personal interaction and communication. Much as we hate to admit, even the audit groups within Big 6 and second-tier accounting firms, where many OCFO personnel cut their teeth before moving into industry, don't stress these competencies as much as they should.

To be fair, finance is not the only area in which companies are finding their new recruits undertrained. That is why companies are increasingly turning to internal "universities," conducted in-house or on-contract with a local college or university. We can only hope that companies see fit to include finance courses in their curriculums and to include finance personnel in their nonfinance courses in operations, marketing, communication, leadership, and teamwork.

In our final chapter, on making the change happen, we'll discuss some of the organizational assessment tools you can use to get a handle on this issue.

Structure

The days of having a pure centralized or decentralized management model are gone, and matrix organizations are no longer in vogue. Instead, most successful finance organizations we have seen since the early 1990s are team-based organizations. This evolving structure appears to have three main characteristics:

1. *Clear, limited corporate functions.* Successful finance organizations have decided the role that corporate finance will play and what the purview of the business unit finance organizations will be. Corporate generally includes such activities as tax, treasury, external reporting, financing, and a small management planning and analysis group.

2. *An SBU focus.* The majority of finance activity has moved into the SBUs. Staff is assigned and dedicated to the SBUs, developed to ensure a deep knowledge of the unique characteristics and value drivers of each SBU, and focused on the business problems and analytic questions facing the senior business unit management.

3. *Shared services for transaction information.* Leading-edge companies have come to realize that the costs of running multiple platforms or sets of financial transactions systems is not only not cost-effective, it is damaging the company's ability to get required information on a timely and consistent basis. The financial transaction systems and processes are, with few exceptions, not core to the business. In order to run them most

cost-efficiently, most leading companies have already moved aggressively to develop shared-service centers in the United States. Lessons learned from these experiences are beginning to move to Europe and Asia, where cultural and other barriers have made the change much slower.

Even with increased autonomy at the business unit level, there is still the need for a pool of leading-edge expertise at the corporate level.

In C&L's August 1994 benchmarking study of global finance and accounting at 17 multibillion dollar companies, we identified two of the most common finance and accounting reporting structures for international operations. In the first, the finance and accounting staff reports directly either to business unit management, with a strong dotted-line relationship to corporate management, or to corporate management, with a strong dotted-line relationship to SBU management. The other has finance and accounting staff reporting directly to regional management, with a dotted-line relationship to corporate management.

Ford and Johnson & Johnson are notable examples of companies that have decentralized many of their larger divisions into smaller units and put the financial people out with operations. These managers often report directly to the presidents and are charged with acting as partners with the business units, and hence they have greater profit and loss and operational responsibility.

Swissair and General Electric are two examples of companies that have not only moved people to the business units, but given them the task of developing business-unit specific information that supports decision and provides advice to the unit on how to improve performance on an ongoing basis.

Digital Equipment, Dun & Bradstreet, and Johnson & Johnson are three companies that have successfully moved their transaction processing into a selected number of financial shared-service centers that will serve the key transactional needs of multiple business units so the central finance staff can focus on value-added or leading-edge analytics. This last point is taken up in more detail in Chapter 6, as are the issues of technology and processes.

Aligning the structure of the OCFO with the overall company is not as simple as picking a model that has worked in other companies. The organization structure for finance should be a function of roles and responsibilities. For example, if the corporate CFO and controller has responsibility for the integrity of processes, finance in the SBUs should probably report directly to corporate. If responsibility for process integrity is decentralized, then so, too, should the organization be decentralized.

Culture

Changes in the character of the finance and accounting functions are grounded in a broader shift in corporate culture. Building a financial community in the face of decentralization has unique challenges.

A strong finance community has a common language, usually the chart of accounts that is reinforced by accepted and well-understood policies. This implies that regardless of reporting arrangements, the organization must be characterized by the corporate CFO playing a major role in the human resource planning for the entire financial community—hiring, performance review, recognition and compensation, and career-path planning. A clearly mapped out career path is especially important if people are being brought into the organization who don't have all the necessary skills. It must be seen as more than just a series of stops so one's ticket can be punched along the way. It must be a well-planned path of development of one's specific skills and competencies.

It is important that the corporate financial community build relationships with other corporate and business unit leaders. Only if there is openness and candor can the relationship work; there should never be financial surprises between the corporate center and SBUs. But this is not enough, the financial community must also create relationships with financial communities in other companies. This will enhance the ability to benchmark and to learn from others' experiences.

Finally, the financial community must be brought together regularly from the business units to share best practices and reinforce their efforts. These meetings should be not only for financial leaders from the business units, but for those who "actually do the work."

Wrap-Up

In the world of the twenty-first century OCFO, there will be no trade-off between efficiency and effectiveness. Rather, there will be a determination that certain parts of the OCFO's function will have an efficiency focus—the transaction processing functions—and that these functions will be ripe for process redesign, shared services, or outsourcing. On the other side of the coin, there will be OCFO functions that will have an effectiveness focus and these functions will need to be reengineered in a way that makes the OCFO a full business partner with the CEO and the rest of the executive team, the marketing organization, and the operational arms of the company at divisional, business unit, and plant level.

3
Strategic
Issues

Leading-edge CFOs are increasingly adding value through direct and active involvement in strategic matters. This is especially true in medium-size companies with no strategic planning department and in large companies where strategic planning and CFO duties are carried out on the business-unit level.

Even in those large companies that maintain dedicated strategic planning departments, the office of the CFO plays an integral part in linking operational data with strategic thinking and providing direction through strategic analysis. Adding value through strategy goes well beyond a compilation of projections, beyond budgeting and forecasting. When the OCFO is integrally involved in strategic analysis, it becomes easier to create performance measurements and management controls that are meaningful in a business sense rather than merely a bookkeeping sense.

From our work with clients in many industries, we believe that emerging best practices in the area of strategy include the active use of external information from consumers, customers, competitors, and suppliers; a growing focus on end-to-end strategic planning across the value chain; a focus on both account and customer profitability; questioning of assumptions and the company's risk posture; and an increased focus on the relevance of assumptions, not merely on the accuracy of the numbers.

At the heart of the strategic portion of the CFO's new agenda is ensuring that the CFO and staff understand the host of analytical tools available to them and deploy them in an integrated program of planning, resource allocation, and ongoing performance measurement throughout the company. Today few OCFOs are using tools like economic value analysis, target costing, competitive cost analysis, strategic cost management, activity-based management, core competency management, and value-chain analysis to their full potential. Where they are using them, that use is too often sporadic and inconsistent.

Figure 3-1 is our QuickGrid reference of the characteristics of OCFOs at various stages of their development as leaders in strategic planning. In order to move into the leading positions, it is necessary for CFO organizations to get beyond looking only at the internal components of the company and to become participants in the external market, competitor, and economic analysis necessary for supporting the company's strategy.

Figure 3-2 shows the distribution of companies along that continuum and the difficulty of moving along the continuum.

Value-Chain Analysis: The Key

A number of CFO organizations are linking much of their strategic work to a clear and accepted value-chain analysis for the business that looks beyond the internal value chain that operations managers usually study in their reengineering or total quality efforts. The CFO is uniquely well positioned for this task. In theory, he or she has the analytic capabilities, the relevant numbers, and the breadth of understanding of the dynamics and interrelationships those numbers show. He or she is well positioned to analyze the value chain for the entire industry, from the company's suppliers through the internal value chain to the customer's

LAGGING	BEHIND	MEDIAN	AHEAD	LEADING
REVIEWER • Unclear strategy • Separate business plans • Separate financial plans • No financial strategy • Review plans for financial accuracy	**SUPPORTER** • Linked but numbers-driven business plans • Separate financial strategy • Provides basic assumptions	**ANALYST** • Integrated planning • Internal value chain analysis • Activity-based planning • Ad hoc initiatives • Produces strategy "Bible"	**MARKETEER** • Positioning relative to key competitors • External analysis and benchmarking • Objectives tied to performance measures	**STRATEGIST** • Formal strategic planning role • Value network analysis • Drives strategic cost management • Changing the industry model • Evolving process • Activist in competitive analysis and benchmarking

Figure 3-1. Comparative positioning on C&L's QuickGrid—strategy.

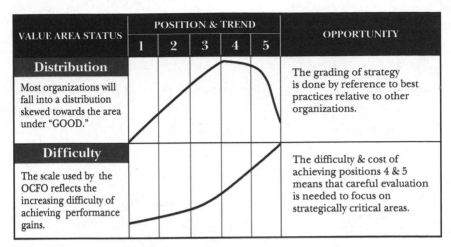

VALUE AREA STATUS	POSITION & TREND					OPPORTUNITY
	1	2	3	4	5	
Distribution Most organizations will fall into a distribution skewed towards the area under "GOOD."						The grading of strategy is done by reference to best practices relative to other organizations.
Difficulty The scale used by the OCFO reflects the increasing difficulty of achieving performance gains.						The difficulty & cost of achieving positions 4 & 5 means that careful evaluation is needed to focus on strategically critical areas.

Figure 3-2. Comparative difficulty chart—strategy.

value chain and even the end user. Although this is compelling, it may also be threatening to many at the executive management level, since it requires the CFO to have access to operational details and marketing assumptions traditionally considered to be the purview of those areas. The key is not that the CFO supplants these groups, but that the CFO becomes another intelligent voice adding a different perspective to the decision-making process.

Michael Porter, of Harvard Business School, was one of the first to define the concept of the value chain in the 1980s. Porter argued that companies need to understand how all of their activities relate to one another within the value chain. Recent work by John Shank and Vijay Govindarajan, of the Amos Tuck Business School at Dartmouth, have furthered the concept of value chain. They argue that each business must view its own value chain within the context of the entire industry's value chain, from raw materials to end user. Each business must analyze its competitors who hold a similar position in the value chain and create an appropriate strategy for developing and sustaining competitive advantage.

Shank and Govindarajan have taken the concept of value chain and shown how it can be extended so that the strategy a company determines from its value-chain analysis will have an impact on the way the company sets up its cost-management system, thus transforming value-chain analysis into an actual tool for decision analysis. It is in transforming the value-chain analysis into another tool that we believe leading OCFOs are adding value to their companies' strategy.

In fact, we believe strongly that value-chain analysis should be the starting point for many of the strategic analytic techniques used by leading finance organizations, as shown in Figure 3-3.

Value-chain analysis can be used to outline strategic options, such as:

- Should the company pursue a strategy of forward or backward integration?
- Should the company aggressively seek new markets?
- Should the company work aggressively on new product development?
- Where along the industry value chain do costs matter most?

Beyond the "10,000-foot level" of strategy, value-chain analysis can also be used to focus discussions on key industry pressure points and issues, such as retail margin pressure, customers demanding more quality for less cost, and inroads being made by private label goods. Because value-chain analysis can also be used to point out key drivers of customer satisfaction, it may also be used to rank order business processes for reengineering.

Value-chain analysis can be a powerful tool for the OCFO to use in

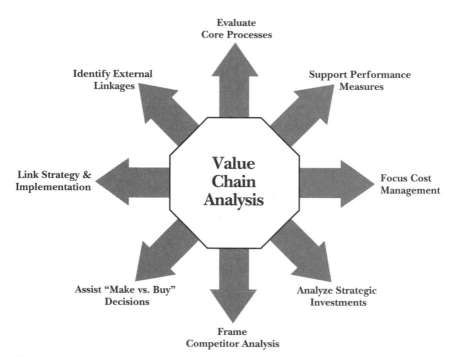

Figure 3-3. Value chain is the analytic starting point.

bringing issues to the attention of the rest of the organization. For example, a large, privately owned meat processor and distributor, a leading supplier to the country's fast-food companies, was experiencing great pressure on margins, combined with an increased need to grow internationally. In starting to examine the company's strategic options, the OCFO developed the first value-chain analysis ever used in the business.

Figure 3-4 shows the particular pressure points identified along the industry value chain.

In subsequent refinements of the value-chain analysis, the company was able to determine what kinds of returns it was deriving from processing and from its distribution activities, compared with companies that specialized in each component of the industry value chain. The analysis highlighted the multiple times raw material was transported to the company. The analysts asked if the company should arrange a strategic partnership with a transportation company given the high cost of transportation throughout the value chain.

The company also began to understand how vulnerable it was to emerging competition from meat packers, who could easily obtain the capital equipment necessary to process meat and chicken themselves into the final product of single-serving hamburgers or chicken patties.

On the customer end of the value chain, the company started looking at emerging retailing formats, as well as other commercial outlets for its products, including schools and other institutions, as a way to decrease its dependence on its largest customers, the traditional fast-food outlets.

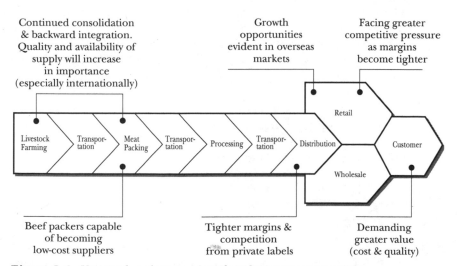

Figure 3-4. Using value chain to identify industry pressure points.

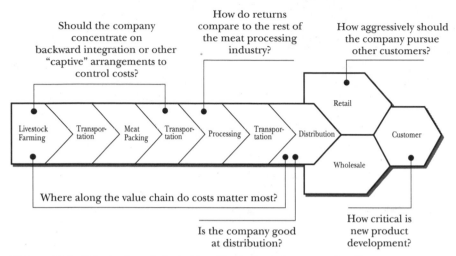

Figure 3-5. Using value chain to identify strategic issues and options.

Finally, when the value chain was looked at end to end, the company realized that its historical position as a value-added (and premium-priced) supplier was no longer viable given the tremendous margin pressures in the current fast-food market. As a result, the company determined that a major cost-management program was needed, and it moved quickly to implement one.

Figure 3-5 shows the end-to-end value chain and the parts of the value chain the company's questions focused on.

As a final demonstration of the power of value-chain analysis, the company used the issues raised by the value-chain analysis to structure its own strategic planning and budgeting process. In fact, we believe that the concepts underlying value-chain analysis can help create the bridge between operational information, business drivers, and the planning and budgeting process, which many companies agree is currently lacking. Companies that use value-chain analysis in order to improve their overall strategic planning are far better prepared to replace the traditional strategic plan and associated budgets with a dynamic performance-planning process, as shown in Figure 3-6.

Planning and Budgeting for Tomorrow

A key way for CFO organizations to break out of their traditional mold and have an immediate positive impact is through innovations in the budgeting and planning process. In most companies, the budgeting process

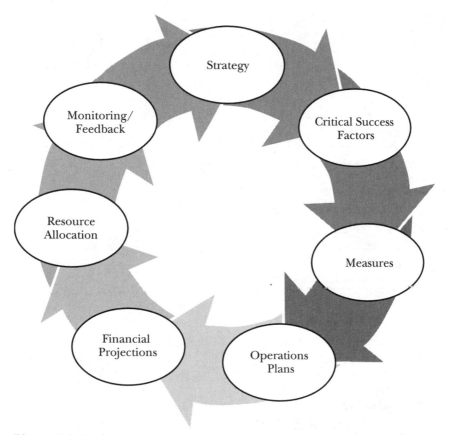

Figure 3-6. Budgets are becoming part of a dynamic planning loop.

rarely serves its intended customers or goals. Ostensibly, the output of the planning and budgeting should serve as a tool for strategic business unit managers, as well as overall guideposts for senior executives and the corporate board of directors. However, too often it is done on multiple systems with multiple sets of assumptions—which might be all right for SBU managers but certainly doesn't help the board very much. At the same time, it is often done centrally from corporate headquarters, which doesn't give the SBU executives enough input into the process.

In fact, the common complaint that budgets and forecasts are excessive in their line-item detail, and either manual or spreadsheet intensive, really reflects the fact that in many companies strategy is, in essence, defined by the budget.

Budget data take far too much time and money to collect. In C&L's 1994 survey and comparable analysis of leading budget practices among 15 companies with average revenue of about $2 billion, no company took less than 3 months to complete its annual budget process. About 22 percent of companies took 7 or 8 months each year! Another 20 percent took 5 or 6 months, and about 60 percent took 4 months. Another study, of 17 global companies with an average $10 billion, was completed in late 1994. It showed similar results. One company in that study actually took 14 months, meaning it began budgeting for 2 years out before the new year even started.

Multiple iterations with executives are often required to clarify assumptions. In the 1994 survey, 35 percent of companies said they went through two iterations, while 40 percent went through three. About 7 percent went through four, and 16 percent more went through five or more iterations.

Now all of these resources would be impressive if the planning process created something of value. But, our experience shows that time and resources that could better be used in the marketplace adding value and generating revenue are instead put to work reworking budgets, adding little or no incremental value. Little time is spent on brainstorming alternative strategic options or testing scenarios against likely competitive reaction.

As a result, the budgets are often unusable, inaccurate, or irrelevant. Much of the data requested for the annual plan is not relevant or usable in running the business. In addition, the process is internally focused, even in businesses where operational activities are increasingly based on external customer and competitive benchmarking. Finally, current planning methodologies often concentrate employee effort on "beating" the numbers in a manipulated plan rather than on improving the business.

Despite these problems with traditional budgeting, we believe that best-practice budgeting can play an integral role in a company's overall management and planning, as shown in Figure 3-7.

Transforming traditional budgeting is a process that involves a series of progressive steps. A first set of better practices includes moving from line-item to activity-based budgeting, increasing the effectiveness of automated systems, and reducing the amount of non-value-adding and manual activities undertaken. These better practices improve the efficiency of the process largely through reducing the time and cost of the annual budgeting exercise; the goal should be to complete the process in 2 months or less. Cost is reduced by using people efficiently, no more than 2 to 3 percent of full-time equivalents within the OCFO. To do this, you need to focus on system improvements. Systems need to be leveraged to reduce manual input while being made more flexible to support data access and analysis.

Better practices focus primarily on making tactical and system

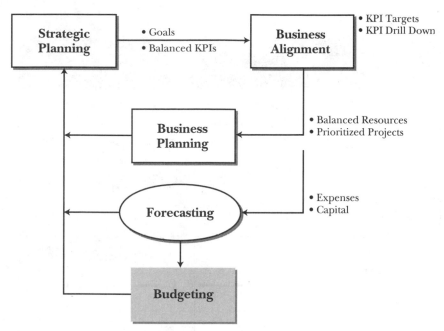

Figure 3-7. Budgeting is a vital link in the overall planning process.

improvements that make the budgeting process better, as shown in Figure 3-8.

By providing different SBUs or business groups with integrated and enhanced data access, you can produce information that provides real insights on trends and opportunities. You can begin to provide a sense of standard, target, and ideal measures, as opposed to only having prior-year budget and actual numbers. This ensures that the budgeting process evaluates means as well as ends and that it evaluates risks and opportunities.

Best-practice tactics, shown in Figure 3-9, continue to increase efficiency by outlining executive expectations that guide the process and ensuring that the planning part of the effort drives the budget, not vice versa. It means changing the focus of discussions and getting explicit agreement on priorities, compressing the formal planning period, and reducing reviews to no more than two iterations, one within the SBU and one at the corporate level.

These best-practice tactics also guarantee that the process can adapt to an ever-changing business environment. You should look to institute a rolling 18- to 24-month plan, linked to the customer-planning horizon. High-level financial modeling tools should be used to develop the

	BETTER Practice Benefit		
Practice	Time Reduction	Cost Reduction	Increase Data Flexibility
Leverage Systems to Reduce Manual Effort	⬤	⬤	
Increase Systems Flexibility to Support Data Access and Analysis	⬤	⬤	⬤
Deploy Systems to Support Modeling and Scenario Analysis	⬤	⬤	⬤
Increase Organizational Flexibility			
Measure Processes vs. Functions			⬤
Integrate with Company Strategy			
Link to Team Performance Compensation			
Focus on Programs, Risks and Assumptions			

Figure 3-8. Better practices in budgeting.

annual plan framework and ensure the company addresses thoroughly its key assumptions and market strategies, as well as likely competitive reaction. Critical to a value-added budgeting process is the framework and the culture that welcomes and rewards critical scenario analysis and business simulation.

Best practices focus on identifying and monitoring the business's value-added activities and processes as well as on linking key performance indicators or new performance measures to team and individual employee compensation. This link to compensation is critical in order to ensure that the behavior created by the plan is consistent with the company's overall goals.

Best practices in budgeting include setting targets at the outset of the budgeting process, implementing a forecasting process to identify changing business conditions and alternative plans of action, linking strategic planning to budgeting, and developing a clear commitment to analyzing competition.

Practice	BETTER Practice Benefit					
	Focus on Strategy	Extract Relevant Measures	Change Focus of Management Control	Capture Correct Data	Integrate Across Organization	Link to KPIs and Compensation
Leverage Systems to Reduce Manual Effort				●		
Increase Systems Flexibility to Support Data Access and Analysis		●		●		
Deploy Systems to Support Modeling and Scenario Analysis	●	●	●	●		
Increase Organizational Flexibility	●		●		●	
Measure Processes vs. Functions	●	●	●	●	●	●
Integrate with Company Strategy	●	●	●	●	●	●
Link to Team Performance Compensation	●	●	●	●	●	●
Focus on Programs, Risks and Assumptions	●	●	●	●	●	●

Figure 3-9. Best practices in budgeting.

While many companies use their monthly forecast as a way to track variances against plan, best-practice companies use forecasts as a way to constantly adapt their 12- to 18-month rolling strategic plan. In other words, rather than try to make the forecast fit the predetermined plan, best practice says the forecast should be used as a tool to constantly fine-tune the plan in real time.

Forecasting is the process of reevaluating business conditions, updating assumptions and operating activity information, and developing short-term action plans to try to meet longer-term planning targets. In essence, forecasting must be used as a tool by which the business reevaluates its performance and plans in light of reality. Too often, the forecasts that companies put together are brilliant examples of spreadsheet and modeling acumen that bear little relation to the market realities facing the business. Leading OCFOs use forecasting as an important way to assess the validity of plans and targets against a backdrop of competitor actions and business environment changes.

Competitive Analysis

Much of the information that goes into a company's plans is readily available—how the economy as a whole is progressing, perceptions of the company's products and services by it customers, market-based data on share and product performance, and operations data regarding productivity and quality. But a key set of information required to improve the overall planning and budgeting process is often the hardest to get—information regarding the competition.

Most companies collect competitive insights on a periodic basis—especially from quarterly published financial results—and competitive evaluations are put together as part of the annual plan. Competitive information that enhances the published data comes from a number of sources, including:

- Sales force reports
- Focus groups
- Customer interviews or feedback
- Suppliers' comments

But it's important to go a step further, to look at companies outside your particular industry who perform similar services; they may be competitors you don't know about at this time. Think of the emerging super-industry of communications and entertainment as an example. In 1985, no telephone company thought of cable television as competition. In 1990 the most savvy in the phone industry were looking at cable television and at the upstart wireless communication companies when they did their competitive analysis. By 1995, the potential rivals of 1990 were very real. The same can be seen in the freight, logistics, and overnight package industries. In 1985 they were distinct, but by 1995 Federal Express, J. B. Hunt, and countless others were all in direct competition.

To get a better and more continuous idea of what the competition is doing requires much more than just an active and involved OCFO; it requires a mobilization by the entire company to keep its ears open and see the implications of those little nuggets of information that do appear. For instance, if a competitor has been touting a new product launch, but then also pushing its old products via aggressive pricing, perhaps the new product is actually being delayed–a fact that could open up an opportunity for your product to be better positioned.

Most companies put their competitive analysis together using one of the many textbook frameworks, all of which start with a structural industry analysis. Our observations show us that if you follow one of these frameworks blindly, you can arrive at a fairly good treatment of the potential in the market, but what is missing is any "personality" of competitors. These rigid frameworks don't give you an indication as to competitors' likely reactions to any of your moves; nor do they give you any feel for a competitor's real intentions or its stomach for a true battle. Also, there is little indication of the competitors' true drivers of profitability. Without this insight, you are often running blind, without any understanding of competitors' organizational capabilities or financial resources.

In leading companies, we see that the OCFO is becoming increasingly involved in trying to put together a strong competitive financial review that can be used to identify those areas of competitor strength and vulnerability that could affect the company's own strategy during the planning period. In doing the competitive analysis, the OCFO is reinforcing its new role as definer of key performance targets and as contributor to strategic questions and scenarios.

With a thorough knowledge of its own company's key performance indicators (discussed in detail in Chapter 4), the OCFO can ask important questions about the competitor information that becomes available. The OCFO is in the best position to collect information and present it in a cogent way, not allowing discrepancies to be explained away. For instance:

- If rework rates are significantly higher than a competitor's, will the head of operations should be ready with an answer?
- If the competitor's sales and marketing expenses per unit are estimated to be 3 times higher than yours, how can the head of sales and marketing in your organization address the implications for your cost structure?

Just as the heads of operating units and marketing organizations have a responsibility to develop a plan of action taking into account this competitive information, the OCFO also has an area where it is required to develop a program of action—against competitive performance benchmarks in the areas of working capital and resource productivity. Increasingly, companies compare their capital structure against their peers in the industry to determine if differences in capital or financing strategies offer a competitive window of opportunity. Completing this kind of peer analysis is usually quite straightforward and can be accomplished quickly using publicly available information and extrapolations about privately held competitors based on the company's ongoing competitive analysis process. Our experience is that all companies should regularly evaluate their competitive performance on several classic dimensions, as shown in Figure 3-10.

Having completed and updated a peer analysis of asset performance, it is critically important for the OCFO to then set targets for perfor-

Profitability	• Sales and Earnings Growth	**Efficiency**	• Sales per Employee
	• Gross Margin	**Liquidity**	• Interest Coverage
	• Operating Margin		• Current Ratio
	• Net Margin		
		Investment	• Capital Expenditures
Capital	• Sales/Assets		• R&D
Management	• Sales/Working Capital		
	• Return on Equity		
	• Cash Flow to Debt Coverage	**Value Creation**	• Projected Growth in EPS
	• Asset Turnover		• Dividend Payout
	• Net Trade Cycle		• Price/Earnings Ratio
	• Days of Inventory		• Market-to-Book Ratio
	• Days of Receivables		• Return on Assets
	• Days of Accounts Payable		• Return on Invested Capital
			• Economic Profit
			• Total Shareholder Return

Figure 3-10. Dimensions to evaluate competitive capital performance..

mance improvement. The targets that are set must be easily understood and capable of being translated into concrete objectives for the various parts of the business. As such, the starting point for the targets and the analysis should reflect how the company approaches the market and utilizes its assets. However, the OCFO can add real value if it uses the peer performance analysis to ask provocative questions.

One example of how important it is to think ahead of time about who the peers really are comes from the CFO of a multibillion dollar high-tech manufacturing and service company. In starting out, the CFO identified about nine major segments of the company's business and structured the analysis along these dimensions, even though the company was organized functionally, with very little segment orientation.

Nevertheless, the definition of these segment-based peers reflected an emerging view in the competitive analysis area that the dimensions of competition were changing in such a way that the company needed to get a lot closer to its customers and rethink its overall approach to the market. When the results of the comparative peer analysis were presented to the executive team of this company it indicated that the company could free up about $338 million annually through better working capital management and potentially redirect these resources to fund a number of strategic projects. But, the analysis was even more important, for it not only opened up everyone's eyes to the potential for significant asset improvement, it also prompted a whole series of discussions regarding the company's overall approach and structure. Beyond getting decent peer analysis, therefore, the up-front integration of strategic value-chain and industry analysis into the data-gathering process played an even more provocative role in the company.

Linking Strategic, Operational and Capital Planning

One of the most important ways CFOs can enhance corporate value is by promoting the consistent use of a well-designed set of financial tools and guidelines to safeguard assets and maintain or even increase shareholder value. This is done by effectively controlling working capital, prudent risk management, and allocating capital through a planning process that is integrated with the strategic planning and budgeting cycle.

The Office of the CFO must assume the leadership role as a manager of the company's strategic resources through its management of the capital resources to ensure they create value for the company. It must not only understand the market, the customers, and the industry dynamics of the company, but also the operational drivers of success, as discussed in Chapter 4. The OCFO must manage the company's resources so there is a clear integration between the changes that are occurring in the market and the company's strategic objectives and competencies.

This is not a new idea. In fact, one can argue that capital planning and allocation is one area where the finance organization is indisputably recognized as having the leadership role. It has always held the final purse strings for the allocation of capital for projects.

Today's CFO must stop thinking about allocating or even budgeting capital and look toward the strategic investment of capital. The OCFO needs to play a key role in the company's strategic decisions through the investment appraisal process by utilizing modeling tools and the ability to think beyond the numbers.

Aligning operational and financial strategies is paramount, and capital projects must be chosen based on the fit with the company's overall strategic and economic goals. Performance criteria are tied to economic results, often using an overall measure of economic profit or value created, such as EVA, to tie it all together. Rigorous risk analyses and evaluations must be applied to old and new business lines.

Leading CFOs are ensuring that the entire process of allocating strategic resources to projects and initiatives is consistent with overall company goals and strategies. In practice this means changing the traditional capital budgeting process, deploying a new program that better integrates strategy with investments, and actively measuring progress against targets.

But what's wrong with traditional capital budgeting techniques?

1. They are often used to justify and formalize decisions that have already been made rather than to objectively evaluate the benefits of proposed capital expenditures. Projections of cash flows can be easily influenced by even the slightest change in key assumptions. The focus on cash flows often makes it difficult to justify or promote projects that have "softer" benefits but that may be even more important in the longer term, such as improved customer satisfaction and retention.

2. The overwhelming common practice of using a single hurdle rate based on a weighted average cost of capital fails to distinguish that some projects may have a level of risk far greater than others.

3. Post-project assessments, while completed by many companies, are not used to ensure that the company learns from mistakes.

4. Finally, many companies fail to hold to the capital commitments that are made. If the performance of one business begins to suffer, all too often the corporate headquarters goes to a strong performer and asks it to make up the difference, through either reduced period spending or deferred capital spending, even if that business is meeting its targets and requires the planned capital in order to sustain its progress against a value-creation program. This leads to increased suboptimization.

This is not to say that traditional capital budgeting is of no value. In fact, over the years many OCFOs have successfully educated the rest of the company in the process of increasingly rigorous investment analysis. Not only is a common language developed, but the technique of evaluating incremental future cash flows does indeed have some validity in an environment where the alternatives being evaluated are relatively similar in their costs and benefits and where risk is really pretty determinable.

Adoption of improved capital planning and deployment and sophisticated risk-analysis techniques, such as decision-tree analysis, Monte Carlo simulations, and probability analysis, can be helpful. However, they are looked on skeptically by operations because they are often not well understood and do not lead to a bottom-line figure, or to commitments, which is the hallmark of the business-case system used in most companies. Also, these techniques generally require specialists with particular skills. This at a time when many companies have been shifting responsibility for business-case and capital-planning requests to the operational managers who will "own" the project. These sophisticated risk-analysis techniques take ownership away from operational managers unless an extraordinary amount of time is taken to educate them.

While these techniques are gaining visibility largely through the efforts of the academic community, via scholarly writing and promotion in the financial press, their use in the real-world corporate setting requires such a deep understanding of the true variables of the decision, as well as its probabilities, that most companies find the techniques very difficult to institute. However, there have been some very high profile users, most notably Merck and Co., led by its CFO Judy Lewent.

Coopers & Lybrand has developed Telesim™, a sophisticated simulation system for the telecommunication industry, which allows companies to consider how and where to deploy technology based on the strategic market responses of competitors. Using some of the advanced approaches developed by the Sante Fe Institute and NASA's Star Wars program, we melded into this simulation model the use of chaos theory and the theory of complex adaptive systems.

This may seem to be a long way from developing strategies and allocating capital, but the large number of companies who now use Telesim™ indicate that this approach simulates the very dynamic and complex telecom market environment. As companies deploy various new technologies into different markets competitors respond. The company must then decide what programs and initiatives to take at what cost and against what expected value.

Telesim™ is just one example of the kind of sophisticated modeling and scenario tool marketing, finance and operations users in leading companies are using to examine the effects of introducing new technologies and the effects of capital planning on market forces.

We believe that as we move into the twenty-first century, companies will increasingly use sophisticated risk-analysis techniques. There are major forces pushing companies in this direction. Our experience shows that these techniques force a company to address the alternative scenarios of risk and be explicit about the company's risk appetite. They also allow a company to become slightly more nimble when something adverse to the plan occurs. The company accepts risk as a given, and rewards people for the strength of their analytics, not for having the right answer.

In most cases since the mid-1980s, companies have undertaken cost-reduction-driven investments where it was relatively easy to estimate the number of people-years saved or how much capacity utilization was increased. For cost-reduction-based projects, the risk was in many ways very low and the results pretty certain within a tolerable range.

But in the future, a large portion of the investments made will be focused on creating the core competencies to support the company in growing its revenue and/or differentiating itself in terms of its servicing, technology, or some other attribute. In these cases, the entire process is really one of game theory—thinking through the options, the alternatives, the likelihood of competitive responses, the level and pace of market uptake, the ability to shelter a market from competitors, and a host of other variables.

Competitors who sense that a company may be conservative in its investment planning and tied to strict capital planning and hurdle rates may aggressively move to preempt and innovate on the basis of quality or service, differentiations that are intrinsically hard to quantify, putting into motion an entire series of market changes.

Whatever classification system a company uses, traditional capital budgeting favors the known over the unknown. There is far more discussion at the senior executive level about the quantitative than about the qualitative aspects of a project. New capital planning and budget methodologies increasingly force more qualitative discussion into the mix.

In some companies, we have started to see a standardization around 15 to 20 key business criteria, which include both tangible and intangible quantitative and qualitative factors, so decision makers can consistently focus on the enterprisewide impact of capital and investment decisions. (It is interesting to note that in companies where new capital planning methodologies are being used, there is an overall effort up front to create performance measurements that are more balanced and integrative, that add nonfinancial measures to traditional financial performance measures. This is the subject of our next chapter.)

These new methodologies also force more central or corporate involvement in the capital planning and allocation process. Senior executives are asked to challenge assumptions and the business case and to ensure that the company looks at the relationships between SBUs or groups and their projects. This central view results in better linkage of strategy and resource allocation.

Ideally, the finance organization helps the SBU leadership build the business case, adding an independent perspective that challenges the as-is assumptions in the business and helps assess risks and probabilities. The OCFO provides an extra set of eyes and ears that ensures that the project truly creates value in a way consistent with the company's overall strategy and risk appetite. In this way, the OCFO can pave the way for the capital allocation request through the senior executive team.

Early involvement also allows the OCFO to be in better position for post-project assessments, an activity increasingly seen as important. Traditionally, such assessments were simple scorecards that rated a project "good" or "not good," using superficial analysis of returns. But learning organizations are increasingly using these assessments as a way to determine where assumptions or conditions have changed since the original business case was created and to identify a process by which such errors in planning and forecasting can be minimized or eliminated in the future.

Linking the strategic, operational, and capital planning process can truly have a transforming effect on a company. It is not enough to define value creation targets in the strategic-planning and operational-planning processes. Value creation is greatly influenced by how resources are allocated to strategic initiatives and then monitored to ensure that value is delivered as projected.

What the Process Might Look Like

Transforming budgeting into best-practice budgeting will require several steps. Implementation paths will be business-specific and use different sets of enablers. But in general there are four steps:

1. Transforming the traditional budget into an activity-based tool that measures the underlying work the organization performs.
2. Evaluating the "value added" to products by each activity or process; not taking for granted costs embedded in previous years' budgets.
3. Matching products with either an internal or external customer to find total expenditures associated with serving different channels.
4. Creating a strategy budget that balances proposed expenditures against company and SBU strategies and goals.

Sometime in July the CEO, CFO, and business unit senior management should get together for a day for the "state of the business unit" meeting. By the end of this meeting, the SBU leadership and corporate executives should have come to an overall agreement on a limited number of key objectives.

Discussions in this early meeting must focus on the business's strategic positioning, the alternatives that can be pursued, and the way in which value can be not only created but maximized. At this meeting the SBU gets its chance to update senior management on the business environment. The chief executive uses these sessions to set the milestones and targets that will define the unit's success and its managers' compensation.

In October, the SBU leadership submits its plan. The plan must outline the appropriate strategic and financial targets that will be met, usually on a multiyear basis. This plan can be less detailed than current plans because many extraneous details have been eliminated and since agreement has been reached in advance on the goals and objectives. SBU leadership does not have to justify in its planning document each of the assumptions it uses to reach its stated targets. But in other respects, this plan is even more complicated. The plan must reflect the resources needed over a multiyear period and be framed in terms of strategic initiatives, not line-item accounts. For many of our clients, this focus on initiative is often one of the hardest to accept because they are more comfortable doing traditional discounted cash-flow-tested capital funding. We do not mean that every project has to be forecast here, but the SBU has to understand and project the group of initiatives it must make in order to achieve its strategy.

Senior management must be willing not only to fund on a strategy basis, but to commit to continuing the funding as long as the business is creating value.

The process just outlined lets each SBU's particular circumstances rise to the top of the discussion. The focus at the early meeting should be on the broad assumptions and business risks each SBU faces. Between the summer and the fall, the SBU leadership can reevaluate those assumptions in light of the top-level targets agreed upon in order to finalize the October plan. In most cases, the plan will need one iteration between October and November to fine-tune some of the numbers or to adjust numbers because of late-season data that has an impact on the SBU's assumptions.

This kind of process only works in an organization where corporate leadership has confidence in SBU leadership to be honest in their assumptions and honest enough to come back in the fall if necessary and say, "Something has turned up in the data we are using that calls some of our assumptions into question." At the same time, corporate leadership is aware of the risks and expectations for each SBU, and if the budget document produced in October conforms to the general agreement made in the summer, it has to say, "This is what I was hoping you would show me," without asking for endless iterations.

Best-Practice Budgeting Adds Vision

Best-practice budgeting techniques provide companies with vision not only on marketing strategy, but also on issues of management control and organizational integration—how different departments are adding value to the end customer or end product.

Best practices derive business measures from business objectives rather than merely from financial reporting line items. These measures ask: Is what we want to achieve good enough? What key performance indicators must we focus on to meet our goals? They focus on the accuracy of meaningful decision support information rather than merely on the accuracy of transaction-oriented data.

Leading budgeting practices focus on creating the correct measures by relating costs to value creation. This is done by identifying and isolating discretionary programs for value-based analysis; identifying budget costs by class or program and not line-item detail; relating resource charges accurately to programs, activities, and value creation; and building activity-based management capabilities to facilitate accurate budget development.

In this way, the new budgeting processes and analysis are focused on the operational root cause, not merely at financial corrective actions. They build controls into business processes and, by sharing responsibility, provide the basis for teamwork. They look for continuous improvement within a consistent understanding of strategy while leaving open the possibility of changing strategy based on reassessment and new forecast information.

Finally, best-practice input from the OCFO helps the company ask questions such as:

- What strategies should we follow in each of our business units to create value every year? (Instead of asking, What effect will the future have on our vision?)
- What will the company look like in 5 years if we pursue these strategies? (Rather than, What should the company look like in 5 years?)
- How will the selected strategies generate more value than the dismissed alternatives? (Rather than, What annual return targets can we meet as a company?)
- What is the right amount of human capital resource to support the strategy over a multiyear period? (Instead of, What did we do last year?)

The focus of the annual plan and resource allocation process should recognize the cross-organizational nature of the business's value-adding activities, and ask the following questions:

- What key performance indicators reflect the business's success in achieving the approved strategic targets?
- Is the resource request necessary for the strategy?
- Is the resource request the most effective way of completing the programs?
- How can the business continue to improve its most critical business processes?

As we mentioned earlier, changes in the way companies plan and budget necessitates changes in the companies' performance measurement. Performance measurement should focus on a few key drivers of success—each reflecting unique business unit characteristics and strategies. Business unit success must be measured against agreed-upon strategies and milestones for that business unit. Whether measurements need to change before the planning and budgeting process is changed or vice versa is an open question. We believe whichever process you begin to change first, the changes must be very closely related and in many regards they must be done simultaneously.

Let's look at how moving toward best-practice budgeting has helped a few companies.

A publicly traded multibillion dollar food and beverage company had a traditional budgeting process that looked 1 year out. The company already had aggressive supply-chain management initiatives that included formation of major supplier and customer alliances, and it had deployed efficient consumer response (ECR) technology, which allowed the company to take a much more active role in inventory management on retailers' shelves and in promotion management. Despite these moves to get closer to their customers, the budgeting timetable and process precluded the company's sales and marketing groups from being able to jointly plan promotions with their customers beyond the end of the calendar year.

One of the company's major retail customers asked what promotion spending was going to be over the next 18 months—the customer's planning horizon. When this question was asked in October, the company said, "We don't know, our budgeting isn't finished." What was not said was that the budget was only for the next 12 months anyway.

Clearly, this was not in the spirit of other corporate and supply chain initiatives. Eventually, the retailer and the company agreed to work out a program on an exception basis. Word got out, and the finance organization changed its budgeting process to be in line with the timetables of its major retailer customers. This meant moving to a rolling 18-month forecast and planning process which is now more reflective of the dynamics in the company's overall industry value chain.

Another consumer products company with more than $750 million in revenue also had a lagging budgeting and planning process despite moves in the marketing area to "get close to the customer" through alliances, ECR, and other techniques. This company was perceived as a major laggard in product development in a market where product life cycles were increasingly short. The company was about to launch several major new products, costing more than $200 million, at the same time it had committed to analysts that it would have an annual growth rate of more than 12 percent—reaching to $1 billion in a matter of 5 years. Despite having set some grand goals and having made major investment plans that in many ways were "betting the company," the company's budget process still worked on demand and revenue first, scrutinizing marketing and promotion programs to the penny, and treated R&D as residual.

Over time the company has changed its budgeting process to an 18-

month rolling process. The focus of budgeting has been changed to address competitive risks and assumptions—including new product development. Each line of business is required to come in and present a "state of the business" review, with an integrated program of not just existing products but also new products, and to show how funding is required of new and existing portfolios of work. Detail line item budget projections have been reduced by more than 65 percent while the overall scorecard that measures success in terms of financial, customer, innovation, market penetration, and quality dimensions has a tighter linkage to the company's strategy.

A third example comes from the world of high tech. A multibillion-dollar computer equipment and services company had a long and traditional line-item-based budget process that started in April and finished in November or even December.

In order to revitalize the business, a new management team was put in place. The company's organizational structure was changed to a mixture of lines of business and industry programs. Capital was very scarce. And because the company had been criticized by analysts, making the earnings projections was critical.

The new management team told the finance organization that the budgeting process simply took too long and added no value. The process was replaced by a two-stage process, using many of the principles we outlined earlier.

In July a state-of-the-business review was conducted, where assumptions and competitive risks, as well as overall corporate growth and earnings targets, were discussed closely. A model of best-in-class for each line of business was used to set competitive targets for earnings, revenue, growth, capital turnover, working capital efficiency, and other parameters.

In October, each business submitted the detailed plan that was based on the agreements made in the summer. In most cases the targets were relatively straightforward, and the only real battle became one of allocating capital to multiyear projects.

At the same time, the company decided to adopt EVA as a measure of economic profit to increase knowledge and awareness of the cost of capital. [EVA (economic value added) is a registered trademark of Stern Stewart and Co. In just a few years it has become the standard bearer for the concept of economic profit or value creation.]

Senior financial management committed to several major cultural changes:

1. Management reporting was redirected to a "dashboard" and balance of key indicators.

2. The historical tendency to halt capital investment of lines making their budgets in order to fund shortfalls of others was reduced. In its place, the company had the OCFO create a much stronger portfolio review process, and the company has begun to shed itself of businesses historically considered loss leaders.

Going Forward

Redesigning the planning and budgeting process will undoubtedly lead to significant cost and time reductions. Our benchmarking has shown that companies that use traditional planning and budgeting methodologies spend about 0.35 percent of sales on their budgeting and planning process and take on average 7 to 8 months to finish the process. In contrast, leading companies spend just 0.02 percent of sales on budgeting and planning, and they collapse the process into 2 to 3 months at the most. Yet even more important, leading budgeting and planning practices can really add value to the business by making sure that the right questions are asked and by providing both corporate executives and SBU managers with a valuable tool, which links the plans to the organization's overall goals.

Wrap-Up

The OCFO needs to have a place at the table in a company's strategy making. The special skills OCFO personnel bring include their analytic tools, which make them the prime candidates to do comprehensive value-chain analysis, and their understanding of financing and capital structure, which makes them the people to turn to when looking for analysis of the value creation consequences of strategy options.

4

Strategic
Performance
Measures

Management control is the area most people think of when they define the OCFO's main purpose. For many years, finance organizations have struggled to produce accurate, timely, and comprehensive financial reports, no matter how complex the business situation. But there is a considerable body of evidence that shows that much of this information is at best irrelevant and at worst misleading. As the role of the finance organization changes, it is no longer acceptable to just track financial numbers and let operations worry about operational statistics.

In many companies, people are working hard, but at the wrong things. There is too much non-value-added work and too much time wasted fixing problems that should not have happened in the first place. Too much time is spent looking backward, trying to create short-term fixes, rather than looking forward and creating an environment in which the company can be competitive. Meanwhile, customer quality and service demands are rising rapidly. Many companies are finding that weaknesses in their traditional performance information make it difficult to deal with such business realities.

The areas of traditional management control are increasingly being integrated with operational and marketing data to create strategic, holistic, action-oriented *strategic performance measurements*. This is at once less and more than the old concept of management control, since it seeks to create value in the future and identify progress toward meeting strategic goals rather than simply measure the past. Under our construct, budgeting and forecasting fall into the area of the financial community's contribution to strategy, and the capital planning portion of management control goes into financing. Strategic performance measures create value over the long term by driving success along three critical dimensions:

- *Strategy.* Performance measures provide an ongoing mechanism for measuring the organization's success in channeling its strategic goals.

- *Processes.* Performance measures provide actionable, real-time data and use targets for operational excellence in critical processes to create the incentives for improvement and proper resource allocation.

- *People.* Performance measures align the objectives of individuals with the overall organizational strategy, ensuring a universal commitment toward common goals.

The question facing today's OCFO include:

Can I add value by providing my colleagues with a better set of measures than currently used? Assuming the answer is "Of course," then: How can the finance organization move from the traditional model of scorekeeping and providing purely financial and retrospective information to a new model of providing forward-looking and insightful measurement and analysis?

Strategic performance measurement takes as its basic tenet that establishing base controls is necessary but in no way sufficient. Management today often works with measures that are overly complex. It is harder to create a set of simple measures that tie financial and operational actions to overall strategy than it is to just measure everything. Strategic performance measurement seeks to create a set of simple, well-thought-out and hierarchical measures.

Cutting through Complexity by Reducing Measures

We have worked with a number of clients that have provided extremely comprehensive financial information within very short periods of time, and we have found that many of these reports have not been used at all by executive management to guide the company's operations. For instance, at Champion International, a $5 billion Connecticut-based paper and forest products company, a team conducting an activity-based costing exercise found that many of the OCFO's regular performance reports were cumbersome and that no one was using them for decision making.

On a monthly basis, Champion was producing traditional actual-to-budget and variance costs for its product. When asked by the team conducting an ABC analysis to justify the reports, the accountants in the OCFO said Operations needed and wanted the reports. But mill operation staff showed the ABC team a smaller set of key measures they tracked separate and apart from anything the finance group asked for. Even though they didn't look at the actual-to-budget and variance reports, they believed their division management used them. But division management said the reports were for the mill. It turns out that 60 to 70 hours per week of OCFO time were being put into reports everyone thought "the other guys" were using.

Over time, the finance organization got in synch with senior management, and today, cost trends are reviewed annually. Success is measured using largely nonfinancial measures: a one-page report that tracks lead time, scrap rates, work in process, customer satisfaction, and first-pass yields.

What Champion's executives found out and did is being replicated by dozens of companies today. C&L's 1994 global benchmarking study, as well as our client work in the area of strategic performance measurement, shows the following trends among leading finance organizations:

- Identify only information that is predictive and actionable.

- Link strategy to operations using key performance indicators.

- Simplify key measures and reporting processes.

- Measure across key processes throughout the business.

- Balance financial and nonfinancial indicators.

- Communicate key values through the performance measures.

- Balance SBU or geographic performance against corporate results to establish managers' compensation.

Measures That Tie to Strategic Decisions

Traditional measures don't tie management actions to business strategy. It is possible to replace wrong metrics with correct metrics to create such a link.

For instance, to answer the strategic direction question, Where are we going? companies in the past have depended on long-range planning, annual profit plans, and monthly budgets. To create a better link, cutting-edge companies are turning to value-chain critical success factors (CSFs), and measuring CSF progress against continuous improvement targets.

To answer the strategic direction question, How are we performing? companies traditionally have looked at monthly financials and plan versus actual numbers. But forward-looking companies are using benchmarked CSFs, trends in their CSFs, and increasingly using a "soft close" model.

For line of business decisions, companies have traditionally used budgeted margins. But today, leading companies are examining their value chain, looking at competitive costs and life-cycle costs.

To move toward a long-term, least-cost structure, companies have traditionally used standards, budgets, and variance analysis. Best-practice companies are using design-to-target and actual versus ideal as key measures.

The important lesson in all of this is that financial management is not what truly drives companies' results. What drives results is how products and services are delivered to customers and how this is translated into sustainable revenue and a judicious cost structure. So if financial performance is the result of operations, it stands to reason that the balance of the strategic business information and the type of analysis that is done by the finance organization should be operationally oriented. Key measures of service, quality, and operational efficiency must be the focus, which in turn can be extrapolated into measures such as working capital turn and inventory turns.

One of the most important trends to emerge since the early 1990s is the use of a measurement of overall value creation or economic profit. The most common measurement of economic profits, economic value added or EVA,™ was developed by Stern Stewart & Co.

Adoption of EVA is leading companies to refocus their performance reporting, investment allocation, budgeting, and incentive compensation schemes to ensure that achievement of targeted value-creation objectives are met. The measure formalizes the belief that *cash is king.* The return generated from the cash and investments made in the business must exceed the cost of that capital.

Translating this into a measure means choosing between several alternative measures, but the driver is the same—show the net impact of the company's cash generation balanced against the company's cash requirements.

The OCFO is strategically positioned to ensure that the organization addresses how it will create value and measures its actual performance. Typically, the measurement and analysis of value creation or economic profit is used to drive companies to:

- Earn more profit using current capital
- Use less capital to earn the same profit
- It can also identify pieces of the current capital base that offer the most potential for EVA growth
- Ensure that new projects expand the asset base for EVA growth

Choosing to use EVA is only the first step. The experience of leading EVA advocates indicates that there are alternative approaches to applying the measure. At Coca Cola, EVA has been a corporate and senior management target; while at AT&T, EVA drives bonuses for all management staff, along with customer value and people value.

From our perspective, the most successful users of economic profit are those companies that adopt the metric, focus their efforts on educating and training operating managers about the drivers, and then tie the attainment of EVA to incentives. Operationalizing EVA means linking the measure to the many process initiatives underway at a company. For instance, EVA can be used in managing assets, as shown in Figure 4-1.

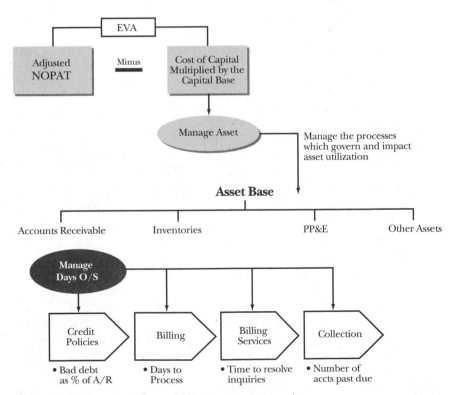

Figure 4-1. Operationalizing EVA in managing assets.

Finding and then measuring performance against the right operational drivers is not as simple as the diagram in Figure 4-1 might lead one to believe. In fact, in most of the companies with which we have worked over the last few years, finding the right drivers means working through three or four levels of measures before finding the one that not only has the most important impact on value creation, but can be measured monthly or even more frequently, and is controllable by the process team and operational management within a company. Let's look at what one multibillion dollar consumer products company did.

While reorganizing its SBUs to reflect that there was a common set of customers and retailers, the company desired a reduction in costs in some core processes. There was an increase in shareholder activism because the company's returns had started to lag the rest of the industry. There was also a belief that the company had become overextended into a variety of businesses that were not core.

The company dedicated a strategic initiative to implement efficient consumer response with its suppliers and retail customers. It institutionalized contribution value as a primary form of analysis to show how assets were being used by each of the SBUs and to ensure that performance improvement programs would have both a balance sheet and an income statement impact.

The company developed a sensitivity analysis by looking at how three major strategic alternatives would affect the company's overall contribution value. The three scenarios were:

1. Reduce cost of capital.
2. Increase net operating profit after tax (NOPAT) by 10 percent.
3. Improve cash management by decreasing outstanding receivables by 25 percent.

Results of the sensitivity study are shown in Figure 4-2.

On an SBU level, the company performed similar analyses and incorporated in their operational planning ways to create more value through earning more profit using current capital, using less capital to earn the same profit, or investing in the highest contribution value projects. Performance reports were refocused on operational drivers of success, not results-oriented financials.

Each of the SBUs were required to ensure that their plans included clearly identified initiatives, as well as measurements against which the effectiveness of these initiatives could be measured, such as capacity utilization, inventory management levels, price protection, cost reduction, and quality improvements. As the SBUs were defining the specific initiatives and their measures, the finance organization worked along-

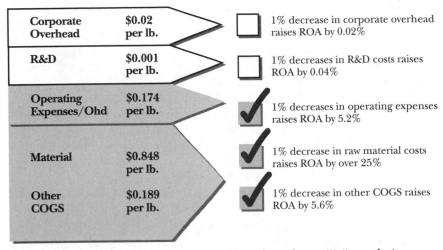

Figure 4-2. Identifying value creation options through sensitivity analysis.

side to ensure that the measures defined could be directly linked with the overall measure of value creation the company had chosen.

In doing so, the finance organization significantly enhanced the company's overall acceptance of the new measurement technique. As a result, when the company decided to introduce a revised incentive compensation scheme that was based heavily on the value-creation measure for both its senior executives at the corporate level and management at each SBU, it was generally accepted. People understood what was being sought. They saw that the measure formed the basis for how the company planned, allocated resources, and measured performance, and now how they were compensated.

Providing the Right Measures at the Right Time

Having defined the company's strategic business information needs, leading finance organizations are aggressively moving to ensure that the performance measurement systems and processes that are in use are linked, consistent, and relevant to the company's strategic vision. What companies often find is that by measuring operations closely and at the process level, then by working to improve operational processes, financial measures improve.

Linked

Management needs a view of business activity that links finance, operations, customers, and competitive pressures. Only by fully understanding the drivers of value, process, and activity performance can they continually strive for improvement. In addition, it is important for executives to see their company through the eyes of shareholders and customers, since the long-term financial performance and creation of shareholder value remains the ultimate measure of business success. Finance organizations that are determined to lead and contribute value must also move to combine this with a continual monitoring of the business and competitive environment so that a company can anticipate change.

This idea fits well with the concept of the *balanced scorecard*, first laid out by Robert Kaplan and David Norton in their 1992 *Harvard Business Review* article. The balanced scorecard is an approach by which a company can see the impact that activities today have on critical dimensions of corporate performance. Three dimensions that are almost always used are financial, customer and internal. The fourth dimension is the one that allows companies some flexibility. Kaplan and Norton used the term *innovation*, although other companies use such variables as growth, employee, or process. The balanced scorecard concept serves to balance a company's short-term financial goals with those objectives that can create long-term value.

At one client, a subsidiary of a global services company, one way the company responded to significant competitive pressures around the world was to overhaul its performance measures. The company examined the detailed business processes and the sources of true value throughout its value chain, and came up with 20 key measures, of which only five are financial in nature. Four major areas were defined, financial, customer, internal, and growth. All of the measures are seen in Figure 4-3. A few words about each set.

Financial.   Three of the five financial measures—EVA, cash flow, and operating income—were identified as most important to the company's shareholders. The remaining two—project profitability and sales backlog—were primarily for management purposes, reflecting which projects were the primary revenue drivers and future performance trends.

Of the five, two are the traditional retrospective measures of operating income and cash flow; the other three are prospective measures.

Customer.   Four customer measures were defined to reflect customer perceptions and the company's competitive position in its customer's view. Results of a customer survey were used to measure at a macro level customer satisfaction as well as to gauge overall brand awareness and brand preference.

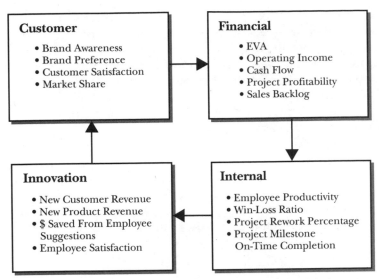

Figure 1-3. Representative "balanced scorecard" for a global services company.

Market share was included as a measure to ensure that improvements in customer satisfaction were reflected in tangible company growth.

Internal. The company defined internal issues as those related to the process of selling, winning, and delivering its products and services. As a result, the four measures in this category reflect how well the company is working with companies to win their business, delivering the project without rework, meeting key project milestones, and utilizing employees as productively as possible.

Innovation. The last major category, growth, is defined to reflect that staff learning and growth are critical to ongoing competitive success. The four measures in the section are intended to drive continuous improvement in the areas of new revenue from existing customers, new service development, employee satisfaction, and the dollars saved as a result of employee suggestions.

Consistent

The now familiar saying, "What gets measured gets done," is critically important for the finance organization. In many companies finance has tended to claim ownership of company measures. But today since strategic measures must reflect not only the company's financial objectives, but the operational goals of each operating unit or SBU and the corporate strategic goals, the role and responsibility of Finance vis-à-vis the measures must be clarified. The "new" Finance organization must become an objective definer of the common business language which establishes a consistent view of the measures. Finance can also add value by ensuring the integrity of the architecture which produces the information required by Operations as it is needed.

The performance measurement processes and the specific measures used must be consistent with overall goals if there is any hope of gaining consistent performance. Key performance indicators focus senior management attention on achievement of the critical success factors. By aligning activity performance measures with business objectives, a company can ensure that the critical activities are the ones that actually get done.

Relevant

Relevant measures must support management by focusing on processes rather than functions. Measuring someone on a discrete part of a process no longer makes any sense. Continuous improvement and learning and development at the process level are key to remaining ahead. Understanding total process performance and the real contribution made by each activity in the process is the key to improvement.

It's important as a final step to make sure these measures are tied directly to appropriate reward and incentive schemes.

Moving from Concept to Reality

Each company's set of particular measures will be somewhat different, depending on the particular business, industry, and competitive position it faces.

For instance, a U.S.-based courier company has taken these ideas and translated them into a revised management by objective (MBO) system for its work teams.

Using the fundamental premise that financial performance is derived from operational and market success, the company has largely replaced its financial measures with a daily look at service quality. Twelve categories of measures have been defined and rank ordered. These measures include missed pickups, damaged packages, wrong-day delivery, etc.

With the category of measure defined, the company then assigned each category a point value. On a daily basis, actual points are calculated for each team. As in golf, the goal is to get the lowest number of points. Teams with a consistently good record are often asked to work with teams that need help to improve their processes. They share what they have found works and what doesn't.

The point system and reporting—both what is good and what is bad—is tied into the team's MBOs, which in the words of one senior company executive, "takes the concept out of the clouds and mixes it with everyday business."

Another way to let critical indicators of operational performance drive the structure of the management reports is to benchmark or do comparison studies. You can benchmark either against those companies you actually compete with in the product marketplace or with companies that produce any product or service but use the same process you do. Remember, you are competing in the capital markets with all companies, not just those you compete with in the product marketplace.

Figure 4-4 shows a comparison study an international textile manufacturer did for a new CFO in the face of declining sales and margins as well as pressure from the company's key bankers. Discussions with major customers identified critical performance targets as they compared to those of principal competitors. This allowed the company to set 3-year goals to improve these key parameters which would hopefully translate to improved market share and margins.

In response to these pressures, the new CFO led a companywide effort to create an improvement program. A major obstacle was that the cause of the declines could not be determined from the traditional cost-accounting systems and management-reporting processes. As a logical

Quality Levers	Weighting	Year 0	Year 1	Year 2	Year 3
Number of Faults	40	140	80	60	20
Non ID of Faults	25	60	44	24	10
Color Quality	15	60	70	90	95
Handle Quality	10	55	75	90	95
Packaging Quality	5	20	60	80	80
Number of Mends	5	50	30	20	10

Figure 4-4. Continuous improvement scorecard for an international textile company.

step to absorb more overhead costs, the company began to increase production. The result was more losses.

To remedy the situation, the company basically threw away the standard-cost system and determined that it had to run the business with nonfinancial measures. An analysis of the company's value chain and operational performance drivers was conducted and overlayed against the information provided in the company's management information reporting package. The critical management performance indicators that were defined included error rates, cycle times, progress in improvement programs, on-time delivery, and order lead times. The company focused on improving various forms of errors.

Armed with this definition of key performance indicators, an analysis of performance against the key drivers was undertaken. It was discovered that only 72 percent of operations were value-added. The majority of work consisted of inspection and rework because of poor quality. Once equipped with an indication of how the company was performing against these key measures, a series of programs was set up with clear targets for improvement, and the improvement was tracked closely.

The company began to monitor and improve its quality through corrective action. Within a short time, cash flow improved, quality increased significantly, and the quality of earnings was improved.

Creating a Set of Strategic Performance Measures

Truly strategic performance measures will go beyond even the balanced scorecard approach. The balanced scorecard is a good framework, but it lacks context. Each company needs to create a customized set of strategic performance measures based on the internal and external value chain while using the balanced scorecard concept as a guide. This will provide the company with a set of measures that looks forward rather than backward and can act as an early-warning system for potential problems.

Creating such a measurement set is a three-step process:

1. Start with strategy.
2. Design the measures.
3. Plan and implement.

This seems like a very clean and straightforward process; but, in reality, it is not simple.

Strategy

A good practice is to use the strategic performance measurement process to identify the need for a well-articulated strategy, and create one. The best practice, however, is to have a well-thought-out, well-articulated, and generally accepted strategy before attempting to design the measures.

The strategy must address specific market conditions and objectives, address key stakeholders, highlight the company's core competencies and core business processes, and have enough focus so the organization understands both its short- and long-term objectives. It must embrace the value-chain concept and take into account both the company's internal value chain and the company's place on the industry value chain. All of this is discussed in greater detail in Chapter 3.

Design

Assume that a strategy is in place or that the drive for a new measurement system has spurred you to create a more highly developed strategy. To link that strategy to the new measures, you must choose a measurement framework. The most common framework for new measurement systems today is Kaplan and Norton's balanced scorecard.

Putting a framework in place assures completeness and encourages balance. A concise framework limits the number of measures to those that are truly critical. The framework creates a basis for management reporting and for the common language so important to successful change in any organization.

Measures should be forward-looking and predictive, and they should provide a basis on which management can act. They need to be relevant, and they also need to be accessible. Given the information system in place or that you envision to be put in place, we suggest that people ask a simple set of five questions to help select the most appropriate measures. The five questions are:

1. Does the measure support strategies?
2. Does the measure support business processes?
3. Is the measure easy to understand?
4. Can the measure be calculated from obtainable data?
5. Overall, is the measure a good indicator of company performance?

The measurement "pie" can be cut in a variety of ways. Figure 4-5 shows how a value tree can be used to link measures directly to the critical performance attributes valued by various stakeholders.

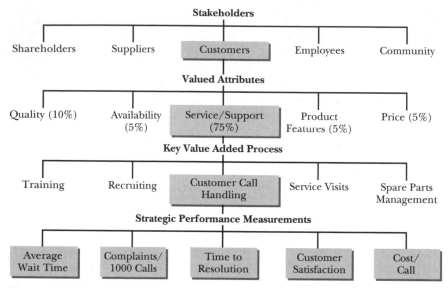

Figure 4-5. Using C&L's "value tree" to link measures to stakeholder requirements.

Figure 4-6 shows how you can link measures across functions throughout a particular step in the value chain or across the value chain for a particular function.

Finally, Figure 4-7 demonstrates a clear hierarchical linkage between those measures by which individual workers may be evaluated up through the organization to measures that concern senior management. For example, to reach senior management's customer-service objectives, lower levels of the organization must recognize how measures that evaluate their activities support the overall objectives. Building from the ground up, you can think of this as the value tree. Or, looking from the top down you can think of this as the value parachute. In either view, the actions taken to affect value at one organizational level have impacts on the measures above or below in the hierarchy.

In order to create a linked set of measures, you need to conduct interviews with key participants in each business process and get them to articulate the key issues, how the process affects stakeholders, how the process affects financial outcomes, the current measurements in use, and any new information that would be needed to provide the new measures suggested. Not only must these new measures be consistent with and support the organization's overall strategy, but they must support consistent behavior across the organization.

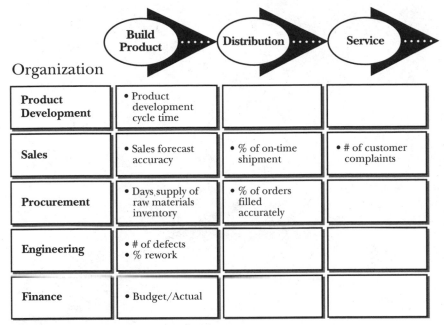

Figure 4-6. Linking measures to organizations across the value chain.

It is important to constantly remind yourself, and all those who you ask for input in creating new measures, that strategic performance measures comprise a limited set of critical information necessary to drive the business, not all the information used to manage the business. Also, individuals at all levels of the organization need to know and be assured that they are responsible for those measures that are applicable in their respective process and at their particular level, not all the measures in the organization. This notion called *span of control* is critical.

Figure 4-8 shows a balanced scorecard framework set of measures we helped one client create, showing overall measures and key measures for organizations within the company.

Implement

The more thoroughly the design work has been carried out, the easier the implementation will be. Measures must be clearly defined in order to gain acceptance. One client created a performance measurement reference guide, which was used both as an implementation tool and as a communication tool.

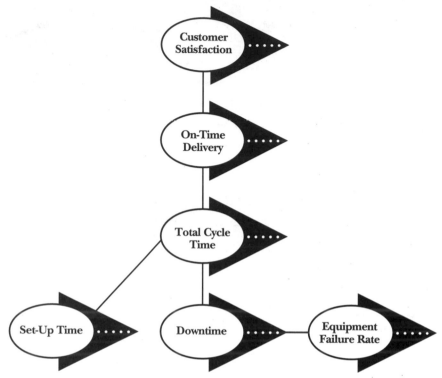

Figure 4-7. Link measures to actionable processes throughout the organization.

Each measure was defined on a separate page, showing the process, the measurement, its strategic significance, the definition and calculation, targets for the first 3 years after the new measure was put in place, frequency of reporting, data sources and ease of availability, the individuals responsible for performance against the measure, and a brief narrative of "considerations" that included issues regarding use or interpretation of the measure and any necessary balancing against other measures.

During implementation, the ownership and use of each recommended performance measure must be confirmed. Effective management reporting is a critical element in the implementation process. During implementation, management should experiment with different ways of viewing the information. Some will want a business summary with narrative; others will want numbers only. Some will want to delve deeply into the numbers; others will only want to do this by exception if there appears to be a problem. Some will want what-if modeling done

	Financial	Customer	Internal	Innovation
Overall	• EVA • Revenue Growth • Operating Income • DSO • Expense to Revenue Ratio • Cash Flow	• Market Share • Willingness to Repurchase • On-Time Completion • Personnel Skills (Training Effectiveness)	• Associate Satisfaction • Forecast Accuracy • Order Fulfillment Speed • Expense to Revenue Ratio	• Hit Rate • Key Project Milestone Completion
Marketing	• Revenue Growth • Marketing Cost/ New Customer • Gross Margins	• Customer Satisfaction • Market Share • Brand Recognition	• # of Distributors and Customers Trained • # Forecast Accuracy	• New Product Line Revenue • Key Project Milestone Completion
Sales	• Sales Force Productivity • DSO • Sales Cost/Revenue	• Reliability Rating • Share of Existing Customer Spending • # New Customers	• # Sales Calls/Contacts • Sales Force Knowledge	• Hit Rate • # Cross-BU Sales Opportunities • Multiple Product Sales • Key Project Milestone Completion
Distribution	• Inventory Turns • Days On Hand	• Inventory Shortfall Avoidance • Order Processing Time • % of installations with correct parts shipped to site	• Inventory Excess Avoidance • Purchase Order Preparation Time	• Key Project Milestone Completion
Service & Installation	• Installation Cost • Service Revenue	• Customer Service Sat. • Service Response Time • Mean Repair Time • Responsiveness	• Installation Timeliness • Installation Quality • Technical Service • Force Productivity • Service Force Technical Knowledge	• Key Project Milestone Completion
Support	• DSO • Cash Flow	• # of bills w/errors reported by customers	• Billing/Collection Cycle Time	• Key Project Milestone Completion

Figure 4-8. Representative balanced scorecard throughout an organization.

for projecting future periods, others will not. Some will want competitor, historical, or market supporting information; others will not.

In reality, there are few, if any, people at any level of the organization
who always know what is needed to run the business. Measures are not
concrete. In our experience at least 20 percent of measures should
change every year as circumstances change.

Today, many executive information systems exist in the marketplace
that can put strategic performance measures at everyone's fingertips.
It's important when looking for software to select the package that can
most appropriately accommodate your business needs and to be careful
not to let the software's capabilities drive the information. The software
must be used as a tool that enables you to create the measurement system you want and need.

Although a strategic performance measurement (SPM) system has
intrinsic value, it must be linked to compensation to be fully effective.
SPM ownership needs to be identified and individual performance
objectives established. Compensation must be linked explicitly to these
individual objectives.

Finally, implementation is not the end. It really serves as the beginning to another round. Because strategy is constantly in flux because of
both external changes and internal conditions, each modification of
strategy creates the stage for a modification of measures that link to that
strategy. However, having said that, we can also say it is almost always
easier the second and successive times around than it is creating the initial set of strategic performance measures.

Implications for the Financial Organization

Strategic performance measurements force the financial organization to
take on a process that has a different set of steps, outcomes, and reasons.
The finance organization must set the business rules through its organization of the business data and its understanding of the financial and
nonfinancial targets versus those of competitors at each step of the
value chain. It must identify those measures that are truly predictive
and determine which people can take action based on those measures.
It must do this while allowing the data to reside both physically and
mentally in the heart of the business unit, not in the accounting office.

This truly breaks the mold of what accounting and the OCFO have been
about since the beginning of the century. Creating an effective office of the
Chief Financial Officer is not simply about cash and dollar precision any
more. It is about making business judgments based on reasonable accuracy and relevance. It is about giving up control of data in exchange for

having more authority over information that the executive management team uses to make the most fundamental business decisions.

Finally, Figure 4-9 is the QuickGrid for performance measures, and Figure 4-10 shows the current distribution and difficulty of moving to the right along the grid.

LAGGING	BEHIND	MEDIAN	AHEAD	LEADING
POLICEMAN • Separate financial and operational measurements • Historic budget process • Variance analysis • Financial targets • Internal focus	**GATEKEEPER** • Structured monthly account review • Bureaucratic processes • Rules and regulations • IRR/NPV analysis • Functional budgets	**ANALYSIS** • Bottom up/top down budgeting • Performance and reward linked • Rapid preparation of results • Comprehensive data • Last year plus %	**SUPPORTER** • SBI/CSF/KPI • Activity based measures • Value-based planning • External orientation • Forward looking	**DIRECTOR** • Continuous improvement targets • Customers perceive value • Integrated capital and operations planning • Real time information delivery • Strategy driven "pull" system • Financial and nonfinancial measures balanced

Figure 4-9. Comparative positioning on C&L's quickgrid—strategic performance measures.

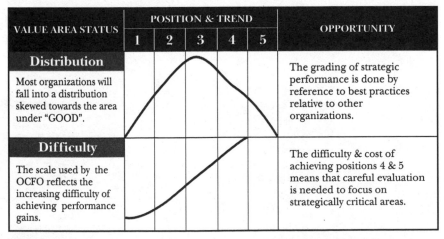

Figure 4-10. Comparative difficulty chart—strategic performance measures.

Wrap-Up

Today's OCFO, through its increasing role as a business partner, is the natural place where a new set of strategic performance measures can be designed. Rather than focusing on financial measures to the most minute detail, the new set of measures must blend operational and customer-focused measures with the truly important measures of the company's financial health. This can most easily be done through use of and customization of the balanced scorecard concept.

5

Strategic Cost Management

A New Context

Today's business objectives are threefold: to make profits, to beat the competition, and to delight customers. To achieve the first two objectives, you must accomplish the third. However, traditional cost-management techniques focused on the first objective only by minimizing cost regardless of the effects on customers. Cost management entails far more than cost cutting.

Leading-edge companies today are broadening their focus of cost analysis from looking simply at the cost of products to looking at costs from a range of perspectives—costs of processes, products, geography, segments, customers, and distribution channels.

They are not only looking at actual versus planned costs within a planning period, but taking the first tentative steps into studying costs over a customer's or product's life cycle. And they are even beginning to see the possibilities of target costing.

As of today, no company has found the key to opening up what we call *the new context* for costing. A big reason for this is that companies are still struggling with whether they have the necessary information to perform the analysis required in the new context; if they have the information, they are finding where within the company it resides; and finally they are struggling over who will take the lead in performing the necessary analysis.

We believe most companies have much if not all of the information they need to perform analyses within the new costing context. Pieces of the information probably reside in three areas—marketing, operations, and finance. Furthermore, we believe a value-adding finance organization is well positioned to take the lead in gathering the necessary information and harnessing it for the purposes of analysis. The OCFO we envision is the fulcrum at which operations, marketing, and the executive suite can leverage the information they possess into a new context of strategic cost management.

However, success demands that the whole organization needs to manage costs. And this means looking at the business's goals in a different way. In the United States, margin is the variable almost everyone looks at, and this is clearly a pretty good determinant of short-term profitability. But the Japanese look at cost in terms of setting targets for cost reduction over the life cycle of a product. This is a demand-pull mindset—the notion that cost management and targeted cost reduction over time, done within the context of what customers are willing to pay, will keep margins firm. In contrast, U.S. companies too often have a product-push or sales mindset—the idea that if products are pushed hard into the market, they will be purchased and the resulting increased sales will keep margins firm.

Since no company that we know of has fully developed the complete set of analytical templates necessary to assemble the important data and analyze it to produce all of the necessary information, the next decade is going to be a learning experience for everyone. The executive suite, the marketing organization, the finance organization, and the operating organizations are all going to have to learn how to do this, and we encourage all of them to learn together.

An important lesson learned by companies that have already begun this process is that sales and marketing personnel begin to truly learn and understand the importance of profitability management, which results in getting them to focus on profitability rather than purely on sales.

This learning should take place in an iterative fashion. The maxim should be "rapid is better than perfect." It will take a number of times going through the data gathering and analyzing process to create the best way of doing it and pull out the most useful information. So we suggest people dig in, do it, do a postmortem on the work they have done, brainstorm about better ways to do it, and do it all over again. In each iteration they will discover new features of how customers determine value and how they can produce acceptable value in a least-cost fashion.

Figure 5-1 is the QuickGrid for strategic cost management, and Figure 5-2 is the distribution and difficulty grid.

LAGGING	BEHIND	MEDIAN	AHEAD	LEADING
BAD COP • Expense category • Functional cost	**HISTORIAN** • Standard costing • Variance analysis • High volume of numbers • Internal analysis • Historical focus	**HIT MAN** • Adversarial budgeting • Cost plus pricing • Zero-based budgeting • Initial process/ activity anaysis	**ANALYST** • Process-based • Cost dynamics understood • Non-Value analyzed and managed • Product focused • Economics overtake accounting • Finance "owns" analyses	**LEADING DIRECTOR** • Target costing • Life cycle cost management • Strategic cost framework • Planned real cost reduction • Customers, segments, geography and product focused

Figure 5-1. Comparative positioning on C&L's QuickGrid—strategic cost management.

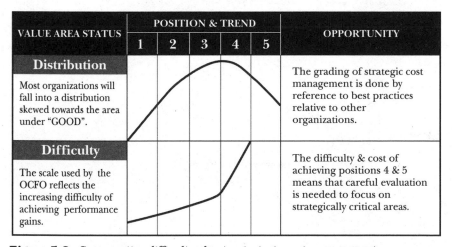

Figure 5-2. Comparative difficulty chart—strategic cost management.

Good cost management must be forward looking. It is still important to look backward, but the more you look forward to target costs and manage operations to meet cost goals, the less you will have to look backward to find out where costs went awry. And thus you should avoid the trap of trying to account costs out after the fact, rather than designing lower costs in before the fact.

The Context

There are four dimensions to the context in which you view costs.

The first dimension is the general mindset. You can view costs in terms of actual costs, planned costs, or targeted costs, or in a combination of two of the three.

The second dimension is the time period you look at. This can be either a budget period, a planning period, or a life cycle.

The third dimension is the process, the way in which the activities are conducted in the business. This is the filter through which the fourth dimension is viewed.

Finally, the fourth dimension is the focus of your analysis. You can focus on products, geography, segments, customers, or channels, or on any combination. The more activities you analyze, the richer your analysis will be.

Figure 5-3 shows the entire contextual scheme, with the ways of viewing costs under the old context highlighted.

The old costing context focused on fixed versus variable costs in a mindset of actual versus budget. It looked at costs within a period versus planned costs. And it focused almost exclusively on the costs of individual products, with slight analysis given to the variability of costs associ-

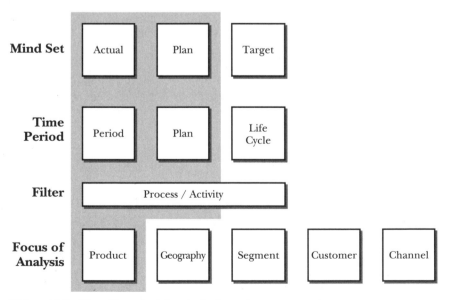

Figure 5-3. The old context for strategic cost management.

ated with either producing or selling in various geographic regions. This narrow context exists because of the use of largely irrelevant tools that have been developed from financial reporting and standard costing. The traditional role of cost management and managerial accounting is based on historical reporting, through (1) standard costs, used to develop inventory costs and generate budget to actual variances; (2) cost to budget information on a natural account basis; and (3) contribution analysis.

However, it is clear to almost everyone that today the conditions that supported these kinds of analyses—long product life cycles, long lead times, minimal technological diversity, and labor-intensive production—no longer exist. Today's companies face global competition, increased product diversity and complexity, shorter product and technology life cycles, capital-intensive production, shorter lead times, and greater customer expectations for quality and service.

As a result, the key questions today's CFO and his or her staff must ask are:

- What tools and techniques should be used to make significant improvements in cost management?
- What are the real cost drivers in the industry?
- How is it possible to tell if we are the least-cost provider? And more importantly, is that important in the segments and markets in which we operate?
- Is our cost-management structure consistent with the company's overall strategic objectives and its key initiatives?

The Intermediate Context: Today's Better-Practice Companies

To address today's challenges, the OCFO must move far beyond traditional standard costing and variance analysis. Figure 5-4 shows a highlighted area we call *the intermediate context.*

This intermediate context is where most of today's better-practice companies are. Activity-based costing (ABC) and life-cycle costing have provided these companies with the ability to take steps in the right direction in terms of costing. This is especially true for companies engaged in process reengineering and redesign. ABC and life-cycle costing are two of the costing tools that have allowed for great gains to be made in companies that are reengineering their processes to increase efficiency and reduce the non-value-added content of their work.

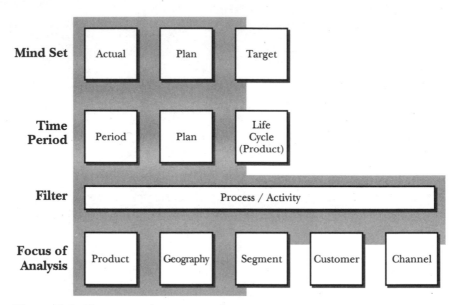

Figure 5-4. The intermediate context for strategic cost management.

ABC has allowed companies to do more rigorous analysis of cost differences associated with production in different geographic areas. In addition, it has allowed them to analyze costs in processes. This in turn has shown how moving toward a horizontal process orientation has reduced costs in many businesses.

Activity-based management (ABM) is a comprehensive approach to cost management based on what activities an organization actually does. The activity level data provides improved information in going to market and in allocating resources. Activity analysis can also identify opportunities for performance improvement to support the drive for continuous improvement. ABM drives companies to eliminate waste, improve core business processes, flex their capacity, and continuously improve the right activities.

Figure 5-5 is a flowchart of a typical ABM process.

These are the key questions ABM prompts a company to ask when analyzing whether an activity adds value:

- Could this activity be eliminated if some prior activity were done differently or correctly?
- Does the technology exist to eliminate this activity?
- Could this activity be eliminated without having an impact on the form, fit, or function of our customer's product?

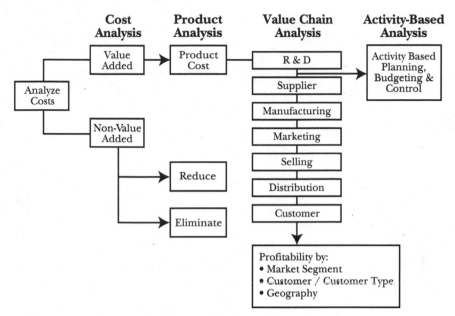

Figure 5-5. Typical evolution of activity-based management.

- Is this activity required by an external customer and will the customer pay for this activity?

Fundamentally, one of the greatest strengths of activity-based costing is its ability to help determine the root cause of problems, as shown in Figure 5-6.

Too often, however, the old costing mindset overwhelms the power of ABM as a tool. Companies look at the information derived from ABM and say, "Aha, look at what kind of analysis we can do with this. Think of how much more we could do if we decomposed the activities down one or two more levels." This is a great fallacy.

An even greater fallacy is to try to collect actual costs by activity and measure them against planned cost by activity. This just piggybacks the old-style detailed control system on a totally different technique. ABM should be used to enlighten strategic decisions.

When activities are decomposed too far, ABM loses much of its value and becomes just another way to drive costing to the level of minutia. Moreover, the effort required to decompose costs further too often leads to the creation of a new bureaucracy and, even more dangerously, to further competition between advocates for different sets of numbers.

What companies that have had success with ABM should do instead is to move to another plane of analysis—strategic cost management. As

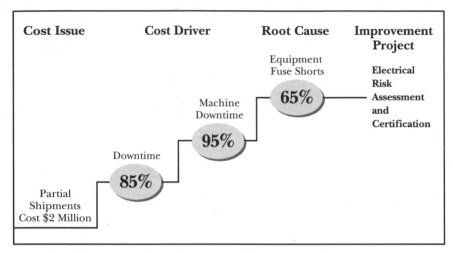

Figure 5-6. ABM supports root cause analysis.

Shank and Govindarajan point out so well in *Strategic Cost Management: The New Tool for Competitive Advantage,* this new analysis extends the basics of ABM by adding value-chain and strategic-positioning concepts to develop alternative strategies for competitive advantage. The combination of value-chain analysis with activity-based costing forces the organization to see itself as part of a linked set of value-creating activities, to let its customer and supplier relationships frame the definition of activities.

By including the concepts of strategic-positioning analysis with the value-chain tools, the OCFO's cost-management efforts can become clearly focused on how the information is to be used in developing strategic alternatives. Cost management thus becomes a constantly evolving tool that reflects the company's strategic goals and vision.

Figure 5-7 shows the case of a large property and casualty insurance company. The company's market breakdown was 80 percent commercial and 20 percent personal policies. The company's overall cost structure was dominated by claims processing, which averaged about 70 percent of costs. Sales, marketing, and administrative expenses consumed about 15 percent, while costs such as commissions and outside counsel made up the remaining 15 percent.

In response to increased competition in the commercial market and decreasing overall corporate profitability, the company reorganized into profit centers for each of its product lines. An on-line system was put in place to assign revenues and costs to specific products and branch man-

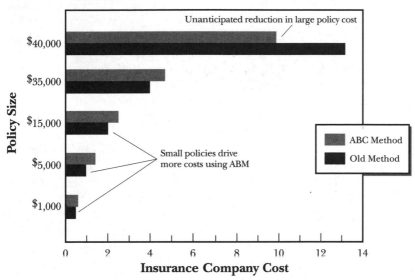

Figure 5-7. Illustrative impact of activity-based costing.

agers. Performance was measured against specific return-on-equity measures critical to the organization's overall profitability.

Although management was satisfied with the effectiveness of the new performance measurement controls, they were unsure of the quality of information driving the cost system and the resulting price algorithms used by the company; pricing was determined using a flat cost of 13 percent for all policies regardless of size.

Many problems existed in allocating internal operating expenses. Activity-based costing principles were chosen as the most appropriate method of looking at the company's cost structure, within the context of not just its internal operations but the overall industry value chain and the different dynamics of the personal and commercial markets.

The results of this study confirmed the shortcomings of the company's cost-allocation methods, which were subsequently being reflected in product pricing. Upon review, processing expenses as a percent of premiums varied significantly, with smaller policies being significantly underpriced and larger policies being overpriced.

As a result of these analyses, management was able to show the value of the tool, the critically important insights it provides for going-to-market and resource-allocation decisions. A series of critical reengineering initiatives were undertaken to radically redesign the entire customer-service and claims-processing activities so that customers' needs were better met while costs were dramatically reduced. This has allowed management to become educated and to transform its view of the cost management system from an administrative burden to a value-creating tool.

As the insurance company found when doing its analyses, today efficiency is not enough. CEOs have reengineered their organizations to the edge of the efficiency continuum. They must now focus on effectiveness and delighting customers as the key to continued growth and profitability. Companies can no longer simply reduce costs all the way to profitability; they must "grow the top line."

Take the merger of Chase and Chemical banks as an example. On the surface, this would appear to be similar to other mergers that were undertaken to create an economy of scale that permits rationalization of operations and cost reduction. But this merger can be seen from another perspective—a rationalization of distribution channels and an integration of customer bases. A power behind this important merger is the potential that exists in the new company's ability to serve customers through a more targeted customer-service capability and translate this into lasting revenue gains and long-term profits.

A competitor quoted in *Business Week* on September 11, 1995, asked, "Can they get the revenue side pumped up with the right focus?" To do this, companies such as the combined Chemical and Chase, must deploy cost-management tools which identify areas of added value and the source of both internal and external cost drivers that mirror the manufacturing and/or service-delivery process and which provide a clear view of how the company's diverse products and services contribute in the long run to profit and the quality of earnings. The OCFO's role here is critical. The OCFO must focus on determining what costs are necessary to the effective delivery to customers of products and services that delight them.

For this, even a tool kit using largely activity-based and life-cycle costing will not suffice. Companies need to get to what we call *value-driven costing*, the ability of a company to cost a value, not an activity. It is this notion of value-driven costing that sets the stage for the new costing context. This is how the new paradigm differs from the traditional cost-cutting mentality:

- Traditional cost-cutting mentality sees administration and support workers as costs to be cut. The value-driven cost-management paradigm sees them as resources to be trained.

- Traditional cost-cutting mentality sees production workers being replaced with automation. The value-driven cost-management paradigm sees them as in need of optimization through technical support.

- Traditional cost-cutting mentality simply sees expenses ripe for cutting. The value-driven cost-management paradigm sees cost drivers that help focus process improvement efforts.

- Traditional cost-cutting mentality focuses on price and variances. The value-driven cost-management paradigm looks at quality, time, service, vendor partnerships, and then at price.

The New Context

A major dilemma in the past has been the difficulty in allocating resources to sales and marketing activity, because there has never been sound, quantitative information that could tell executives how much of a return can be expected on dollars spent in these areas. It is now clear that resources should be allocated where customers perceive the most value to be. But this is easier said than done.

It can be confusing trying to sort through all the relevant costs and methodologies for identifying costs: product costing versus customer costing versus channel costing; activity-based costing versus standard costing versus target costing. We have developed our vision of the new context with the hope that by looking at how decisions are made regarding cost along three dimensions—mindset, time frame, and analytical foci—you can create a matrix for each costing decision that points you in the right direction with regard to what tools and techniques, and what costing methodologies, to use.

Figure 5-8 shows the new context in its entirety. We have drawn a highlight box, however, to show you that the new context integrates target costing in the mindset dimension with the traditional actual and plan. In the time-frame dimension, the key to costing in the new context is life-cycle costing, rather than the traditional period and plan costing.

Mindset

The question of viewpoint is rather straightforward. *Actual* looks at what costs are actually incurred. *Planned* looks at the costs that are assumed for a particular planning period.

Targets are the costs you *want to achieve*, given the mandates of the markets and competitive pressures. Target costing takes into account a number of factors beyond costing. It is predicated on price, quality and functionality, and the trade-offs necessary to create the optimal combination.

Target costing is an approach that first determines the specific product functionality and level of quality required by the market, along with

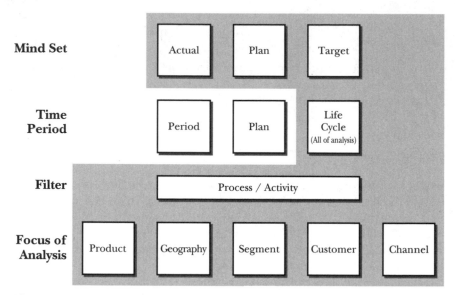

Figure 5-8. The new context for strategic cost management.

the market's willingness to pay, and then determines the product's cost, based on the requirement to generate a needed level of profitability at the market price. Unlike standard costing, target costing focuses on the reduction of costs during the design cycle. It is more strategic in nature than it is operational. In target costing, the product's cost is not a given; rather it is the dependent variable resulting from decisions made with the independent variable's functionality, quality, profit, and price. Figure 5-9 shows the basics of target costing.

The most recent, and perhaps the best, description of the power of target costing is that supplied by Robin Cooper in *When Lean Enterprises Collide.* From our perspective of reinventing the office of the Chief Financial Officer, one of the most important considerations in adopting target costing is the dynamics that have to occur to harness that power. To develop accurate target costs, there must be active communication among the marketing, engineering, purchasing, and manufacturing communities, with the finance organization acting as facilitator. The target cost is the result of strategic decisions made by organizations other than finance. Finance serves the critical role of being the linkage among the parties in determining the end result—the target cost.

First, the finance organization must work with marketing to determine the product's target price. Then the strategic planners must be consulted to determine the target margin.

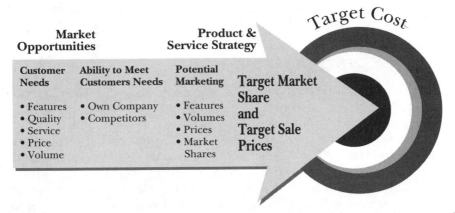

Figure 5-9. Target costing changes the perspective of the company.

Second, the target cost is broken down into its component and raw material pieces. This requires consultation with purchasing and manufacturing managers. The target cost is then determined by subtracting the target selling price from the required margin, which is set by management.

But beyond the role of integrating or linkage, the finance organization must be ready to play another important role. A key philosophy in target costing is that the target cost can never be exceeded. It serves as a sensitive balance between a specified level of functionality, a market-driven price, and a strategic margin. If the target cost is violated, this equation loses its balance. This is where the OCFO's role as referee or honest broker comes into play. The OCFO must ensure that the company's commitments are adhered to. It is up to the parties that worked together to set the cost structure to come together and make decisions so that the target margin can be achieved.

It is not all right to miss the target cost. But it is not the OCFO's responsibility to fix any problems that might cause the agreeing parties to do so. If the targets keep being missed, that's a clear indication of the organization's lack of discipline. In this case, it is the responsibility of the entire executive management team to stop, rethink, do some more preparation, and try it again.

Marketing determines how much customers would pay for a given functionality and quality, and the design group determines how to meet these needs for the target cost.

Target costing is a powerful tool because leading-edge companies are coming to the realization that the best way to control costs is not to incur them at all. The best way to do this is to design costs out of the product or service before it is created, rather than to try to reengineer them out after the fact.

Time Period

Most companies that are doing what we call *better-practice* costing work today are applying the concept of life-cycle costing. *Period* costs look at the costs incurred in the reporting period. *Planned* costs are the costs that are assumed will be incurred in the next reporting period or planning period. Traditionally, this is defined as a calendar year, but increasingly companies are moving to an 18-month planning period, and even an 18-month moving period, which is the intermediate step to life-cycle costing.

Life-cycle costing looks at the costs that are assumed to be incurred over a given lifetime. *The key to understanding life-cycle costing is to see costs as investments rather than as period costs.* Each year, companies such as IBM, Ford, or Tambrands make substantial investments in their image and awareness in order to build preference and a stream of revenue. Not only is this awareness built over time, but the revenue stream is also expected over time.

On a product basis, life-cycle costing looks at the product's cost from the time it is initially conceived through its market withdrawal or significant reformulation. Looking at product costs on a life-cycle basis is critical because research has shown that over 90 percent of costs are committed *prior* to the inception of operations or market launch, as seen in Figure 5-10.

Because cost commitments or commitments to the platforms that dictate long-term cost structure are often made far in advance of when the expenses are incurred or the cash spent, the traditional OCFO and executive management focus on performance of products on a period basis is critically flawed. If you scrutinize costs after operations begin, you are not affecting the real decisions that are made about costs. You must look at the time period in which costs are determined. A leading-edge OCFO must be involved with the R&D personnel early on in the design process so the relevant costs can be analyzed and the product can be designed for cost-effective production.

There are seven stages in the life of an investment—analysis, startup, entry, build, maturity, decline, and withdrawal. The OCFO must use the costing process to reflect the cumulative effect of each of these stages. The leading-edge CFO must use the costing process to provide information to support such decisions as: abandon existing product and replace it with a new design; develop two products in a marketplace at the same time and delay introduction of one product so it does not cannibalize revenue from another.

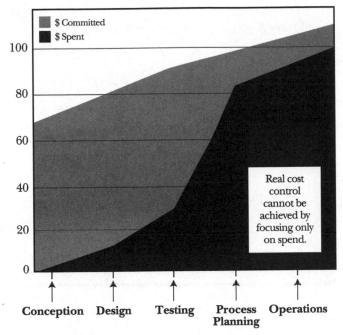

Figure 5-10. Importance of looking at costs over their life cycle.

But besides looking at life-cycle costs for products, truly leading-edge companies are beginning to apply life-cycle costing concepts to analyze their customers. We'll discuss this when we discuss costing as it relates to customers later in this chapter.

The Filter

Costing the process is intended to find the costs at each step of a business process as it goes horizontally through the company. As we mentioned earlier, activity-based costing really does a good job at this.

One key concept here is *process value*, which looks at the value added or not added at each step of a process. Part of the task of process-value determination is to assure that the company maintains the perceived value of its products by *making appropriate trade-offs between functionality and cost*.

This requires that teams made up of people from the finance, engineering, manufacturing, and purchasing communities, as well as suppliers, examine the quality, functionality, and costs. The purpose of this exercise is to determine whether costs are achievable. This happens primarily at the design stage. This then continues through the life of the products to see which non-value-added activities can be wrung out of the process.

Focus

The most common dimensions on which costs can be analyzed are product, geography, segment, and channel; and finally, costs can be analyzed on the most important dimension—the customer.

Product. Product costing is usually the first, and often last, focus of any company's costing effort. The history of accounting literature is full of standard approaches to product cost accounting. But as we discussed earlier, we are beginning to see a slow but consistent shifting in focus to one of target costing and value engineering.

Geography. In almost all companies, revenues, costs, and even some level of profitability are tracked along a geographic dimension. Costing by geography is different from company to company. It may refer to geographically dependent costs of a distribution company or to different buying behaviors in local markets. For instance, retailers or consumer-goods manufacturers differentiate their promotions, leading to far different marketing costs in different regions.

Segment. As a first attempt to get closer to the customer, many companies have undertaken efforts to track revenues and costs for logical groupings of customers who are defined by their similar needs or profiles. While these groupings can take many different forms, market segmentation is like mitosis in biology: the cell has a tendency to split into ever lower levels of disaggregation. This results in a host of revenue recognition and costing issues if the company has old, hard-to-fix legacy systems. For example, your local telephone company's first pass at segmentation many years ago was to group its customers by a standard—the size of monthly bills or the number of telephone lines. A good start, but too internally focused. It described what effect the customer has on the company, but did not describe the customers themselves. A next pass at segmentation might be to group customers based on their intensity and patterns of use: e.g., international calling intensive, professional, local calling intensive. In the future, the next pass might disaggregate the customers one more time, by interest: e.g., traditional local intensive but strong cellular users. This might be a way to focus promotions and service offerings of perhaps certificates for cellular usage.

Regardless of a company's disaggregation or segmentation of customers, the costing system needed to support these kinds of disaggregations needs to become progressively more sophisticated to identify differences among these groups.

Channel. These costs are associated with the selling vehicles the company uses to address its markets. For example, any successful consumer product company tracks its costs for sales made through its own stores versus through retail stores that carry its products or through catalogs, megastores, and shopping clubs, etc. There is more to channel cost differentials than merely differences in freight and selling costs.

Progression through the Foci: The Customer Is King

No company has all the foci clearly thought out to the point where it can do a comprehensive cost analysis of products, geography, channels, and segments. However, there seems to be a natural migration that occurs as the sophistication of the OCFO increases and the marketing and operating organizations feel comfortable working with the OCFO.

A key trend in marketing today is toward target marketing. For many companies 20 percent of customers represent 80 percent of profits. For instance, 2 percent of car renters account for 25 percent of cars rented. In long-distance service, 15 percent of customers consume 60 percent of long-distance services.

Increasingly, marketers are placing a premium on the ability to identify the most valued customers. Marketing expenses may not be reduced with target marketing, but they are more effectively allocated for maximum effect. Database technologies are used to track the effectiveness of promotion programs.

Three key questions need to be asked to foster a more urgent focus on customer costing:

- What customers does the company value?
- What do these customers value?
- What is the customer cost versus the product cost?

The intent of customer costing is to determine costs that are customer driven, whether they are at a customer level for businesses or a customer-group level for consumer marketing. The traditional way to look at customer costs is to view them as period costs associated with expenditures made this year on promotion and advertising. A more appropriate view is that costs invested in customers are cumulative over time.

An investment made early in a customer's life cycle may not be profitable when compared to the revenues derived that year. But if you look at the cost/revenue relationship late in the customer life cycle, the investment may prove to be very profitable.

The clearest example of this is probably the heavy promotion of credit cards and telephone calling cards by companies like American Express, AT&T, and banks to college students, despite research that shows college students to be bad credit risks. By managing the customer relationship closely—starting with low credit limits, not renewing late payers, and continually offering more credit and better terms to students who turn out to be good customers—these companies create customer loyalty and large profits over the lifetime of the relationship.

Credit card companies pursue college students not because of the immediate revenues they produce, but because some of these young adults will be very valued customers in the future if the company can foster loyalty. Credit card companies have taken customer life-cycle costing and profitability management probably as far as any companies in the United States. They encounter large promotional costs to obtain new customers. They group customers into "vintages," by what time period a customer was obtained in or which promotion obtained the customer. Then they assign the costs for obtaining that group of customers. Finally, they track the costs and profitability over time for the group as a whole.

Any of us who received our first credit card during or shortly after college remembers that the credit limit was low, and we often had to have a parent cosign, even if we were employed. How many of us still have that first credit card? Plenty! And what about the first card issued by an association we belong to? How many still have those, even though we haven't been a member of the National Accounting Students' Association for 15 years? Plenty, again!

The keys to success in using life-cycle costing is to understand that the attractiveness of a customer can change dramatically over time and over the life cycle of the customer relationship, such as in the hypothetical case of customers of a credit card company. The company must determine the net present value of revenue by determining the length of time it anticipates the customers will use the card, the servicing costs that will be incurred, and the level of balances customers will roll over.

If we assume that the company has been equally efficient in attracting each of its four customers, you can understand the fallacy of looking at customer profitability as a snapshot or a point in time. Any one of the customers may not be very profitable at any specific point in time, but, in the long run, all of these customers may be very profitable.

Which Customers Should
the Company Value?

Examining the customer base may cause some companies to ask the unthinkable question: Would we be better off losing market share but increasing our revenues by increasing our share of "the best" customers?

In order to answer this question, it is necessary to define which customers are the best. *Best* is defined as "the most profitable." But most profitable over what time frame? It is necessary to go beyond seeking out today's best customer. It is necessary to determine who the most profitable customers will be in the future.

To determine life-cycle customer profitability, the OCFO will have to work with marketing to examine the investments the company is making in acquiring, retaining, and stimulating customers. These costs are not expenses; they should be viewed as investments because they have a longitudinal effect.

To reiterate, there is a natural continuum for how companies advance in the sophistication of their costing models. Most companies start with a focus on product, which is natural. They move from standard costing to ABC techniques. If they are also working toward a process orientation, this complements the reengineering and process redesign work they are doing. From there they either move to geography or segment. Then they may analyze channels. And finally, as companies move from looking at internal activities to external drivers, the focus begins to be placed on customers.

This finally allows companies to break the old mindset, which treated product costs as part of asset creation, while it treated customer costs as an expense to be eliminated. This new mindset asks that customers also be treated as assets and that the customer relationship be treated as something worth investing in. This forces the creation of a mechanism to measure value created by customers over the long haul. Therefore, it is not relevant to do customer costing analysis except on a life-cycle basis. If you do it on a short-period basis, your focus will be on what you'll get, not on what your customer will get. More and more companies are looking at what we call the *business services model* of customer relationships—the first job of which is to create a customer relationship, because it is only through repeat business that true profit will be derived.

An example is helpful. Prior to divestiture in the early and middle 1980s, all of the major telephone companies did their costing primarily to support regulatory pricing. After divestiture the companies were under competitive pressure for the first time, and their initial costing focus was on products. As they got a better handle on the cost drivers for their products and compared their prices with those of competitors' products, they began looking at the processes within the company that causes these cost characteristics. The focus then moved to the internal processes by which they connected with customers, namely the channels, which logically led to more of a focus on market segments, which was also fostered by a maturation in the marketing organization to segment its market more finely. This finally led to the understanding that the primary focus must be on the customer and determining which customers are most profitable and what they value about the products.

What Do Customers Value?

In order to make low-profit customers today into highly profitable customers tomorrow, companies need to determine what about a product or service these customers perceive as valuable.

Much has been written since the early 1990s about the value chain. But one aspect of value-chain analysis that has not yet been fully examined is the issue of what each segment of the value chain contributes to a customer's perception of value. This search for what customers want, need, desire, and would be delighted by has so far been left to the qualitative judgments of marketers. But there are techniques available to begin placing some quantitative parameters around this aspect of revenue enhancement.

Management often has a difficult time assessing whether the marketing and sales cost is appropriate to the revenue returned. The value-cost context allows the company to quantify the effects the company is having on the customer and the investments that the company should be making in customers and products. For instance, the best way to answer the question What is the effect of the sales force vis-à-vis an increased advertising budget? is to determine how customers value the contribution of each.

What customers value has over time come to be seen as arranged around four attributes—image, product, service, and price. Increasingly, nonmonetary value points within the product and service attributes are paramount with customers—reliability, product functionality, service quality, and timeliness and convenience. Customers have an expectation of price based on advertising or sales promotion, but that price does not always match their view of whether the product is worth its price. The value view is often related to the image—an Andersen door or window as opposed to a comparable door or window manufactured at local lumber yard; a Chrysler as opposed to a Plymouth, even though the two car models sit on the same chassis.

Quantification of the relative value customers put on different aspects of your product or service can come from customer satisfaction surveys, image valuation, advertising effectiveness studies, and your own customer life-cycle analysis. As a caveat to those for whom this is a key business issue, don't rely on your standard customer satisfaction survey to get you this information. The key here is to identify those touch points that truly correlate to increased loyalty and retention: Is it billing or courtesy or knowledgeable personnel who avoid transferring a call around like a hot potato?

You must search hard to define the touch points that are truly linked to improved retention and hence to long-term customer profitability. All of this input must then be weighed against marketing costs for promotion, advertising, customer care, and selling.

It has been many companies' experience that when they go through major cost reductions or process reengineering, there is a major reduction in revenue and sometimes there are major service or product failures. That is because too often the cost cutting is done without first answering the question "What will be the effect on customers?"

This points up a key weakness in many organizations: They do not have a good handle on what their customers truly value vis-à-vis their products, and they don't know the key customer touch points within the value chain itself.

Let's look at how one major high-technology service company went about determining what about its products and services customers actually valued. Like other organizations in the industry, the company started with a focus on the largest pools of costs to identify where process reengineering and cost reduction efforts could be deployed. However, before embarking on a lengthy business process reengineering effort, the company stopped and asked of these large cost pools: which of them affect the customer the most? which processes do the customers report are the most important to them? And how will cost reduction or reengineering affect customers?

The company conducted an in-depth analysis of the relationship between customer satisfaction, customer loyalty, and eventual customer retention. Then it segmented business processes and identified those areas of the processes that touched the customer and which of those areas were of highest value to the customer. The next step was to determine how satisfied customers were with those areas. With this information, the company selecting a strategy for reengineering each process was able to reduce costs and maintain or improve customer satisfaction. At the end of 2 years, the company had successfully reduced its costs, restructured its operations, and retained and even improved customer value. Over time, the company expects these changes to increase its customer loyalty and retention rates, and hence to improve its revenue stream and guard its revenue levels.

On a more theoretical level, let's look at Figures 5-11 and 5-12.

The example described by these graphics shows a company that has a particular customer value profile. Customers value its service feature the most (60 percent), followed by the product functionality (20 percent), then price (15 percent) and finally image (5 percent).

Service Process Flow

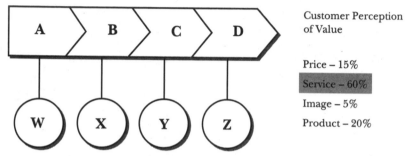

Figure 5-11. Defining customer touch points and value perceptions.

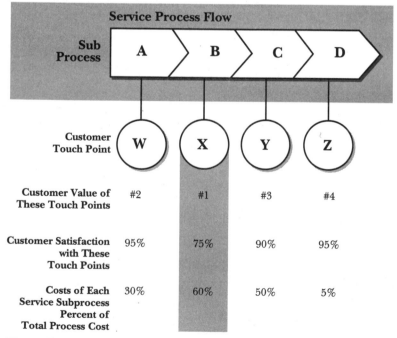

Figure 5-12. Balancing process costs with customer value.

With that in mind, the company should focus its efforts on determining which of its processes both touch the customer and are valued. Next, the company determines how satisfied the customers are with those touch points. Then the company identifies the costs associated with each of those process segments.

In this example, activity *B* is the most important touch point in terms of customer impact and the lowest in terms of customer satisfaction. The art here is to develop initiatives that will improve customer satisfaction and, if necessary from a competitive standpoint, reduce or at least maintain the costs.

This ability to determine what investments should be made in a customer, based on *the customer's priorities*, requires a degree of integration and partnership between the OCFO and the marketing, operations, and service organizations that few companies have mastered.

Costing Migration

While it is easy to say that customers must be examined on a life-cycle basis, we recognize that most companies don't have the kind of costing information they need to analyze their relationships with various customer groups. This understanding of customer-related costs must be grown over time. There is a logical migration companies can undertake to get to customer costing. The migration takes companies from activity-based costing to customer life-cycle costing. Each step along the migration has information limitations, and these must be understood so the information is not used inappropriately.

When companies begin to take a determined customer focus, they find that the information they have available about the customer is rudimentary. Often the only information available is the revenue generated from certain customers. If they are lucky they have some physical sales volumes. This is what they must use for their first cut at customer clustering.

The next logical step is to associate the revenue information with what cost data exist to create a vantage point on customer contribution or profitability. Adding demographic information or purchasing profiles allows a first-cut view of scenarios on how customer contribution might change via more effective target marketing. But the progression should not stop there. Companies must then begin to focus their marketing and sales efforts on the true profit potential of existing customers and on the profitable customers their competitors have as well.

For the finance organization, this has important implications regarding its responsibilities in costing, revenue accounting, and loyalty projection.

- Decide what customer groups you are interested in and make sure source transactions are coded, capturing data at the required granularity.
- Make sure key process costs are also captured at the appropriate level—promotions, commissions, claims, etc.
- Identify as many customer-specific costs, such as bad debt, as possible.
- Track activity over a selected time period that makes sense for the business. This could be 1 year or 5 or even 10 years.
- Use revenue and costs to get a profit figure by customer.
- Examine the churn on your customer database. What is the longevity for customers in a particular segment? Remember, longevity equals more profit.
- Complete a net present value analysis.
- Play scenarios on changes in the variables: costs, revenue, and retention.
- Start all over again.

As marketing and finance work more closely on customer costing and revenue accounting, they will find that they are searching for exactly the same information. With the advent of sophisticated data warehouses being used by leading-edge marketing organizations to support customer targeting, both organizations will find that many of the characteristics of both revenue and cost will be resident in one database.

Companies addressing the need to create these major databases are finding the financial community asking whether there should be just one large data warehouse or separate data warehouses for operations, finance, and marketing.

The separation approach reflects the old mindset of many organizations, and especially financial groups. They want to separate financially related systems from the rest of the company's systems so that they can more easily ensure financial information integrity. But this approach of separate data warehouses runs counter to the effectiveness and the efficiencies that can be provided by modern technology. It may be that the most effective way to structure these systems is to place all the responsibility for revenue accounting systems under marketing. Although finance's proper role is to ensure the financial integrity of this information; it does not mean that the finance organization has to control the system.

As the boundary between finance and marketing fades, the marketing organization will also find that the finance organization plays a more active role in quantifying the revenue and customer lifetime numbers to ensure integrity.

A Few Closing Words

As the OCFO's relationship with the marketing operation and the executive team becomes more of a full business partnership, it is increasingly important that the OCFO develop a large tool kit of increasingly sophisticated costing tools that make the costing decisions meaningful for different audiences. There are a number of lessons to remember as you move in this direction:

- Provide information that is meaningful along the many dimensions required by the business.

- Balance the value of the detail required or requested or that you would like to provide in the best-of-all-worlds scenario with the cost and complexity of acquiring and providing it.

- Recognize that different costs are used for different questions: e.g., cash-based for valuation, accrued for financial reports, economic for pricing.

- Support day-to-day business modeling.

- Provide a common language for decision making: e.g., what is meant by contribution margin or by gross margin?

- Provide an information base that can be used for several different processes: e.g., budgeting, decision making, organizational accountability.

- Use causal relationships as much as possible.

- Measure performance with avoidable and controllable costs; do not allocate that which has no economic or causal relationship.

- Worry about that which is material and forget the little stuff.

6
Processes and Systems

If the Office of the CFO is to truly support the business processes, it must work to optimize the effectiveness and efficiency of the financial processes. Only by making the fiduciary and transaction tasks necessary to any financial operation as efficient as possible can the OCFO free up the resources necessary to carry out the new agenda.

Emerging best practices include measuring processes in terms of resource usage, cycle time, service levels, and other value outputs, as well as integrating financial and operating systems. For instance, purchasing and accounts payable should be integrated, as should billing and accounts receivable, logistics and inventory, and human resources and payroll.

It's important to remember: you can't do it all. You can't drive for effectiveness without ensuring efficiency. But you can't put all your effort in driving for efficiency, or there is no energy left for the work on effectiveness. Only when a company's financial operations are well controlled can the finance organization begin working on the "fun stuff." What exactly does "well controlled" mean? *Well controlled* means adhering to the guiding principles of process redesign and process improvement:

Having an end-to-end process orientation.

Building transaction system reliability and integrity.

Using well-defined policies and procedures.

- Organizing the financial community around a common vision.

- Segmenting the finance function by type of process and activity: making the efficient back office distinctive from the effective business participant.

- Building controls into business processes, and sharing the responsibility for controls.

- Building controls that are cost/benefit justified related to business objectives; aiming at understanding, preventing and mitigating undesirable risk.

- Having easily understood and available information.

- Analyzing in terms of business values, assumptions, and risks.

While a process is a set of linked activities that take input, transform it, and create an output, core business processes are those few processes that are responsive to external events and customers. Value-adding processes add value to the input while transforming it, so as to drive a key aspect of the business. Non-value-adding processes simply take an input, move it around, and re-create it as an output without adding value.

Distinguishing Processes

We have said that as much as 80 percent of the OCFO's traditional activities may not add value to the business. This is a very high percentage, but it is not as extreme as might at first be expected. Similar percentages of non-value-adding activities can be found in many service and production operations.

This does not mean that financial processes can necessarily be eliminated. It does mean that the organization needs to distinguish between the four broad categories financial processes fall into:

- *Identity Processes* define what the company is. There are no financial processes that would be considered identity processes.

- *Priority processes* are related directly to the delivery of services and products. A few financial processes may fall into this category, such as billing.

- *Background processes* support the company with the necessary infrastructure. Most financial processes fall into this category.

- *Mandated processes* meet requirements determined by external bodies. SEC and other reporting requirements fall into this category.

In many cases, business processes operate without financial input, which is only applied at a later stage—for example, in new product development. Financial processes are usually designed to provide checks and controls over business processes, and as a result, add a layer of bureaucracy and complexity. Only rarely do traditional financial processes add value to the business operation.

Despite the seemingly endless stream of criticism about financial processes, they are not irrelevant. To be effective, however, they must be closely integrated with the business and, more importantly, focused on those business processes most critical to the organization. It is probably in areas where the finance organization is currently not contributing that the most gains can be made, by refocusing the OCFO attention. However, if the finance organization is to have time to contribute in these critical areas, it must first become more efficient in the areas that do not add value but that take up a great deal of time and effort. This means taking a hard look at the types of activities undertaken by the OCFO and starting to eliminate non-value-adding processes.

Key financial processes such as risk assessment and financing will generally stand alone, while others such as costing, disbursements, and investment allocation will be deeply integrated within the core business processes of R&D, manufacturing, distribution, and sales. Other financial processes, such as payroll, management reporting, and consolidations/book closing are candidates for redesign, elimination, outsourcing or shared services that will make them more efficient.

Figure 6-1 shows our QuickGrid regarding processes, and Figure 6-2 shows the distribution and difficulty.

Link Financial Process Strategy to Value Drivers

Core financial processes are identified through their link to core business processes and key business drivers. As anyone who has been involved with a reengineering effort knows, a business's objectives drive its strategy, which when combined with the company's core competencies and the industry value drivers, in turn drives the company's core business processes. After identifying these core business processes, the financial processes that are key to the success of core business processes should become evident.

For instance, in the telephone industry billing is a priority process; it is an essential data run that gives the company all kinds of information. In the cable industry, billing is a straightforward background process that cable

LAGGING	BEHIND	MEDIAN	AHEAD	LEADING
• Functional silos • No key drivers • No activity maps • No strategy link • No value analysis • Conflict	• External reporting processes • Control emphasis • Duplication of activities	• Processes owned by functions • Activity-based cost allocation • Some cross-functional links • Initial benchmarking by activity	• Mapping of core business process • Interactive OCFO and operations • Strong cross-functional links • Value-driven networks • Wholistic benchmarking	• Active architect of efficient processes • Focus on core competencies • Business processes orientation • Embed financial process into business • Continual renewal of processes • External benchmarking and networking

Figure 6-1. Comparative positioning on C&L's QuickGrid—processes.

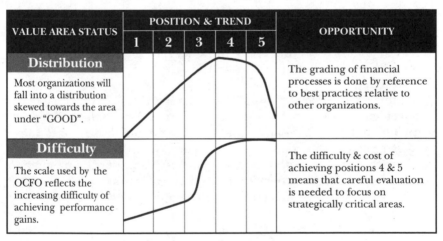

Figure 6-2. Comparative difficulty chart—processes.

companies have looked to outsource. A company called IBS/Cabledata is the largest cable billing service. Now, the phone companies are looking to IBS/Cabledata to perform the non-value-added portions of billing, because the company can do it much more efficiently, allowing the phone companies to concentrate on the value-added portion of the billing and try to create identity processes that tie billing to marketing.

In another example, Johnson & Johnson believes that global cash management is a priority process, creating real value for the company. For many companies, global cash management is a background process, something that must be done in order to do business around the world but doesn't really add much value on its own.

Benchmarking

You can assess the overall current performance of your OCFO through key benchmarks. Measure quality by staff turnover rate per year and training costs per year. Measure service by the number of staff per $1 billion of revenue, the number of staff as a percentage of total company employees, and the amount of effort spent on transaction activities versus analytic activities. Measure cost by the OCFO cost per $1 billion of company revenue, cost as a percentage of G&A/administrative costs, and the cost per employee. Measure time by the time (in days) it takes to complete a credit review or to notify the field of a credit decision or to process adjustments.

Benchmarking as done by many companies today is fraught with difficulty and flaws. Companies collect the data and too often make process decisions without putting the data into the context of what is trying to be accomplished. Successful benchmarking is far more than data collection.

Benchmarking, which targets strategic issues, roles, and processes for improvement, is purposeful, externally focused, measurement-based, information intensive, objective, and action-oriented. It is used to identify best practices to support value creation, to enhance performance against both customer expectations and industry standards, and even to leapfrog the natural cycle of change and improvement.

Although benchmarking is an old concept, it gained acceptance by American corporations in the early 1980s when Xerox created a rigorous benchmarking model that looked at what it would take to maintain competitive parity and what it would take to challenge current industry leadership. With the creation of the Malcolm Baldrige Award, benchmarking increased in popularity, to the point where by 1995 about 95 percent of Fortune 500 companies are using benchmarking.

Comparison of how the process actually works in your company with how it is done in best-practice companies provides a context to the metrics, highlights performance gaps, and identifies opportunities for improvement. A number of basic principles can be used to simplify business processes and create a continuous loop of improvement: stan-

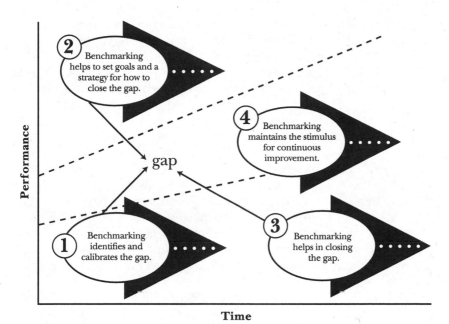

Figure 6-3. Benchmarking offers many benefits.

dardize, consolidate, adopt best practices, link to systems, and constantly evaluate and update. Figure 6-3 shows a number of the benefits of benchmarking.

Benchmarking can be conducted against other parts of your company, direct competitors, the industry in general, or the "best in class." If doing best-in-class benchmarking, be creative when thinking about what "class" you are in—what exactly the process involves and what other organizations use the process. For example, a leasing and fleet management company made site visits to Federal Express, an emergency (911) operation, a travel agent, a bank, a mortgage company, and a brokerage firm to get a sense of where they stacked up against these wildly disparate organizations in such areas as vendor partnering, interactive remote order entry, electronic data interchange (EDI), payment of production, electronic funds transfer (EFT), and knowledge-based systems/client-server systems.

For benchmarking to be successful as a part of a long-term improvement plan, an organization needs to have a company culture that accepts new ideas, executive sponsorship and support, a mindset of continuous improvement, and a culture that allows for employees to challenge traditional assumptions and make improvements.

Challenging traditional assumptions can also lead to best practices in (1) financial processes (such as elimination of paper chain approvals in disbursements), (2) use of electronic media, (3) elimination of traditional financial controls in purchasing (by integrating purchasing, receiving, and payment), (4) reduction of financial information in reporting (replaced by use of key performance indicators), (5) replacement of traditional budgeting with strategic targets and use of focused, targeted budgets, and (6) replacement of the monthly close with a "soft close."

For example, in the area of purchasing, a leading auto manufacturer reengineered its purchasing system to eliminate virtually all traditional paperwork and bureaucratic controls. Purchasing receipt and control of supplies are integrated and controlled by operations. Suppliers are paid on receipt, eliminating the need for invoice matching. Further refinements are being made, with the eventual plan to pay all suppliers based on cars made; when a car comes off the assembly line it has with it a complete bill of materials, listing the vendors and how much they are owed for the parts of systems used in the car.

The work so far has resulted in an 80 percent reduction in necessary personnel for accounts payable. However, to get this far has meant putting in time and effort creating supplier partnerships performing quality studies, instituting rigorous in-process controls, and developing ways to manage expectations.

In the area of reporting, the controller of a leading worldwide consumer goods company stopped producing a "key" financial report that required a lot of manual intervention and rework. Nobody asked about it for 5 months. Eventually, the controller asked a manufacturing plant what was being done with the report. The folks at the plant thought the report was something the finance organization used and that the plant received as an informational copy. The finance organization thought it was something the plant management wanted and used. In its place, finance and plant management came up with a 1-page report of 20 key indicators that were truly helpful for the plant to have on a monthly basis.

A leading global specialist textile manufacturer developed a set of key performance metrics to monitor progress in a turnaround situation that would determine its survival; not one of them was financial, all were directly related to meeting customer needs for quality and timeliness that could lead to developing a competitive advantage.

In budgeting, a leading pharmaceutical company, having reengineered a number of operational processes, then targeted its annual budgets for staff reductions at corporate headquarters; the result was a reduction in the total time required for the budget process from 174 days to 60 days.

The Soft Close—Maybe
Even the Virtual Close

Much has been written about the key purchasing, payables, and payroll transactions that companies are working on making more efficient to reduce costs. Now there is an increasing focus on faster availability of strategic performance measures and a streamlined budgeting process, which we discussed in Chapters 3 and 4. In this regard a key process for achieving control is the soft close.

The sanctity of the traditional financial reporting mechanism of the monthly close is under attack from all fronts. Initially driven by the need to provide detailed financial information for external investors and the perceived needs of senior management, almost all of our clients agree that the the monthly close is a time-consuming, non-value-added, and expensive process. As operations move toward greater use of non-financial measures, the weaknesses of traditional consolidations and financial reporting are being exposed.

There are three approaches to the improving closing process: a hard close, a soft close, and a virtual close.

The *hard close* efficiently performs the steps required by the SEC and generally accepted accounting practices (GAAP) for monthly reporting. In the *soft close,* you do only those steps necessary to produce the information necessary to run the business. In the *virtual close,* systems are so advanced that no closing process is necessary, as a close can be achieved instantaneously, at any time.

Why do we call the soft close a best practice? First, it focuses on the information most critical for management decisions and performance measurement. It eliminates non-value-added time and effort, significantly streamlines and speeds up the closing process, eliminates unnecessary information and promotes informed analysis. The soft close improves the usefulness of data, better balancing the relevance, accuracy, and effectiveness of management reporting. It also matches systems to operations, providing only what management needs when it needs it.

Performing a soft close can help achieve an average 40 to 50 percent reduction in closing cycle time. This, in turn, promotes other best practices, including TQM, external-focused, and a cost-management culture. The soft close also helps enhance necessary internal business controls and eliminates ineffective and unnecessary ones.

Improving the closing process is a continuum, with the first step being the implementation of improvements to the current hard close. These improvements are shown in Figure 6-4. The next step in the continuum is the transition to a soft close. Some of the soft close tactics are shown in Figure 6-5. The ultimate long-term goal of a continuous improvement

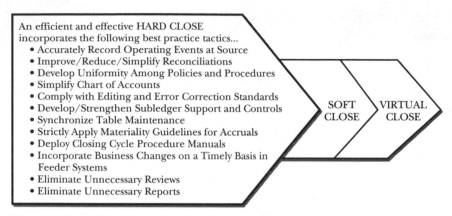

Figure 6-4. Making improvements to the monthly hard close.

Figure 6-5. Improvements supporting a transition to a soft close.

effort in the closing process is the deployment of a virtual close environment. Some of the virtual close tactics are shown in Figure 6-6.

Where Should You Start

To move to a soft close, you must create the environment to support it in terms of:

Controls

Information

Continuous improvement discipline

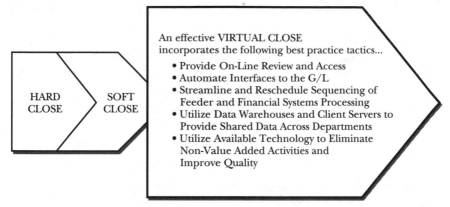

Figure 6-6. Tactics supporting a virtual close.

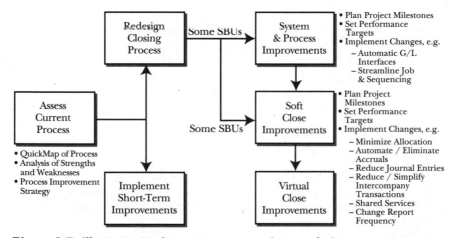

Figure 6-7. Illustrative implementation approach to a soft close.

An end-to-end process view

A soft close does not mean simply stopping many of the cumbersome and manually intensive activities now done and doing them only on a quarterly basis. Achieving a soft close means doing more up front in order to do less later.

Figure 6-7 shows how you might phase in implementation of the soft close in an organization with a number of business units. By having small groups of business units tackle discrete parts of the implementation, then trading the successes back and forth, you can go further faster than with a more traditional rollout approach, where you entirely redesign the process, then pilot it, then move it to other SBUs.

One key to success is mapping the original closing process. A QuickMap of each subordinate process supports identification of key flow points and issues, and also provides a baseline set of information about the process owners, cycle time, and activity distribution. Out of the process analysis and mapping, each company must commit itself to address the primary drivers of activities, effort, and overall complexity that have been built into the consolidation and general accounting activities.

Common drivers of effort and complexity include:

Volume of transactions, especially intercompany or transfer pricing policies and transactions

Detail carried in the general ledger coding structure

Management reporting requirements

Inadequate feeder system controls and quality

Matrix of managed entity and legal entity reporting requirements

Number of managed entity changes and reorganizations

Lack of direct user information access

Lack of user information access skills

Moving to a soft close requires the adoption of a continuous improvement effort in which each of the subordinate processes are evaluated against five overall readiness criteria and process-level performance measures that have been established and tracked.

A number of criteria must be met before the OCFO is ready to create a closing process in which there is transaction system and feeder reliability. They are shown in Figure 6-8.

Figure 6-9 shows the readiness criteria that must be met in order to

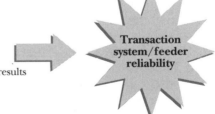

• Availability of Feeder Information
  - All feeders identified
  - Feeder postings scheduled and monitored
  - Feeders analyzed as they are posted
  - Management requirements for feeder
    information are documented and tracked
    (what feeders and what time intervals)
• Variance of key driver predictions from actual results
• Feeder errors are identified and monitored
  - Root cause analyses are executed
  - Corrective action on root causes is executed
    and monitored

Figure 6-8. Soft close readiness criteria—transaction and feeder system reliability.

- Availability of required information (key drivers)
- Variance of key driver projections from actual results
- Number of days from Group and Business Unit
  G/L feeder cut-off to prepare management reports
- Customer perceptions of timeliness of information
- Analysis cost as percent of total process cost
- Number of adjustments required to initial close results

Figure 6-9. Soft close readiness criteria—strategic performance measure availability.

- Number of days from initial feeder cut-off to flash results
- Number of changes to initial results
- Number of days from initial close to final close
- Number of days from final close to management
  information reports
- Variances of key driver projections from actual results
- Process costs as a percent of revenue
- Ratio of elimination entries to total entries
- Ratio of adjusting entries to total entries

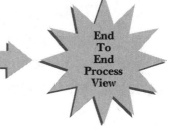

Figure 6-10. Soft close readiness criteria—end-to-end process view.

create within the closing process the availability of strategic performance measures. Figure 6-10 shows what must be tracked in order to create an end-to-end process view. Figure 6-11 shows the criteria that must be met in order to show organizational readiness and to reduce reporting complexity.

Companies that have effectively moved to a soft close have reduced the cycle time of their closing by 40 to 50 percent while eliminating unnecessary information and focusing on information that leads to predictive and prescriptive analyses. The effectiveness, accuracy, and relevance of management reporting are enhanced and controls are also enhanced. In total, monitoring the business performance against key operating statistics helps identify the overall readiness to improve the closing process.

As with any other organizational change, moving to a soft close needs buy-in and commitment from everyone involved in the process, starting with top OCFO officials and operating managers. Effective measurements need to be developed from the beginning, and employees must be rewarded for changing behavior and making progress toward the goals even before the goals are fully reached.

- Adherence to defined closing cycle procedures
- Adherence to closing cycle schedule
- Elimination of root cause problems
- Tracking of feeder system performance

- Availability of information (key drivers) during the month
- Number of errors in feeder postings
- Number of days to prepare management reports
- Customer perceptions of timeliness of information
- Customer perceptions of value and reliability of reports
- Inter-unit transactions as percent of total entries

Figure 6-11. Soft close readiness criteria—organizational readiness and reporting complexity.

As with everything we are stressing, the goal is to focus on directionally correct and accurate information, rather than on exact and total accuracy. Replacing management's view of the world from one centered on the income statement and balance sheet with one focused on a more linked and relevant set of measures—the balanced scorecard, for instance—is often a difficult barrier to overcome. Another challenge is overcoming the fear the financial staff may have that the soft close will redirect resources to different tasks they don't have the proper skills to perform.

Systems and Data Warehousing

A data warehouse is a common database, complete with translators and standard and network interfaces, that allows for input of financial and operational information and output of management and financial reporting and answers to queries. Implementing a data warehouse requires augmenting the current information template with data about key customers, employees, and process value drivers.

Adopting a soft or virtual close requires that the OCFO make key decisions about its systems architecture, the primary purpose of which is to help the business answer its key questions and meet key external and compliance reporting requirements throughout the entire financial reporting process. But because external and compliance reporting is often what is driving a change in systems, most businesses need to address and reexamine the type of common language required by the business and the role of its general ledger.

Legacy systems must be communicated within the same common language requirements, and data warehouse technology will often be required to provide management with the flexibility it requires to gather management information and provide reporting. Leading financial organizations are deploying data warehouses to provide the operational and financial information their users require to make appropriate business decisions.

As shown in Figure 6-12, a data warehouse becomes a critical part of any architecture to support the business in its management information requirements by integrating financial and nonfinancial data and producing meaningful management and financial reports outside of the traditional book close process. Effective use of a data warehouse maximizes the value of the general ledger and minimizes the level of detail maintained. Each of the three components of the architecture—the general ledger, the data warehouse, and the particular applications software used—have a clear role to play.

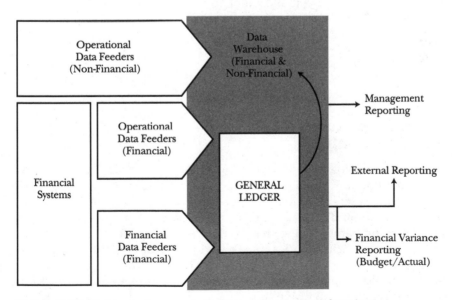

Figure 6-12. Data warehouse role in financial systems architecture.

The general ledger should be used to house the information that is required for external, regulatory, and tax reporting. The data warehouse, on the other hand, should be the primary source of management reporting that combines financial and nonfinancial information.

As much as possible, you must move to standardize and simplify your processes and codes. But don't try to force a standard software onto each operating unit of the company. It may be easier to have multiple standards—one package for business units with certain size or complexity characteristics, another package for business units with other characteristics, and still another standard package for business units with other characteristics.

C&L's 1995 global benchmarking study indicated that there are several common themes in financial system and architecture use among leading finance organizations:

- Legacy systems are out of date.

- Major system implementations are under way.

- The number of general ledgers is being rationalized.

- Shared services is an increasing reality in the United States, while it is further away in Europe.

- New systems have special codes for automatic capture of nonfinancial information.

- Separation of financial and management reporting via a data warehouse is rapidly being accepted.

Figure 6-13 shows the QuickGrid for systems, and Figure 6-14 the distribution and difficulty.

Shared Services as a Key Ingredient

Strategic technology deployment should follow from the organization's assessment of how it will compete in the market. Companies wishing to be product leaders need to focus resources on development and market research costs and consider outsourcing parts of manufacturing and logistics. Companies that wish to be the low-cost leader should focus on manufacturing efficiency, leaving the primary responsibility for promotion to the retailer. Companies that wish to be the customer-service leader should focus on sales, marketing, and customer-service areas and offer buyers comprehensive service.

LAGGING	BEHIND	MEDIAN	AHEAD	LEADING
• Aging systems • Data locked in applications • High maintenance costs • Poor match with user needs	• Poor integration • Unused functionality • Low use of technology • Legacy systems • Rigid operation procedures	• Mainframe system • High use of PCs and networks • Duplication of databases • Inflexible and expensive to change	• Modern hardware and software • High correlation with user needs • Business wide IS strategy • Good use of technology in the company • Emerging data warehouses • New applications under review	• Client server technology • Flexible architecture • Data management strategy • Responsive • Continuous development • Full data warehouse deployment • New financial applications in use

Figure 6-13. Comparative positioning on C&L's QuickGrid—systems.

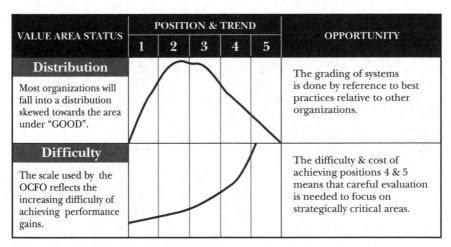

Figure 6-14. Comparative difficulty chart—systems.

The effectiveness of the OCFO can be increased by employing information technology that reflects the business unit drivers and develops generic skill centers as well as by developing special skill sets that support cutting-edge businesses at the SBU level.

The efficiency of the OCFO can be increased by establishing shared transaction-processing services and balancing cost with customer-defined service levels.

A *shared service*, by definition, is an organization that provides common services to operating locations and business units. *Shared* versus *centralized* reflects a shift in power and control to the operating and business units. With the operating and business units in control, shared service organizations must compete for business based on cost and quality.

Financial transactions and accounting must be differentiated from decision support. Decision support will continue based on the customer's needs. Financial management and staff will be able to devote a greater amount of their time and attention to business decision support once they no longer are distracted by daily problems of accounting and clerical operations.

Shared services provide a number of benefits:

- Greater than 50 percent cost reduction
- High quality
- Reduced cycle time
- Quantum productivity improvement opportunity
- Increased employee effectiveness
- Improved management information

The shared services concept is an attempt by decentralized companies to mitigate the explosion of overhead cost from duplication of support functions across the company. The cost of decentralized financial operations has historically been 200 to 300 percent higher than centralized financial operations. Unwilling to accept higher costs, GE in 1983 began to operate under a new model where accounting transaction processing operations were centralized.

Decentralized business units were strong enough to demand return or retention of finance functions that could not be adequately served by shared services. For instance, GE returned general accounting to the business units. Recognizing that viability of shared-service organizations is dependent on customer satisfaction, cost, and performance have become a major focus of annual pricing negotiations.

Getting started in the shared-service environment is a real challenge. Historically, centralization has been viewed as corporate control and poor quality. The personal computer movement in business, for instance, was a revolution against centralized data processing operations. Customers must be assured that they are in control of service requirements and associated cost trade-offs.

Shared services should be established as an independent business. It should have a board of directors, an operating charter and vision/mission statement, a dedicated customer-service representative or team, and a contractual agreement with customers based on service and cost, where the customer determines the cost and service trade-offs and service levels are monitored.

By leveraging systems investments, shared service organizations can take advantage of state-of-the-art technology. Performance breakthroughs of shared service organizations have included automation with customers and suppliers through EDI and EFT, full integration with customer and supplier systems, and standardization of systems and data architecture.

Figure 6-15 shows the steps in a successful shared-service implementation strategy. As shown, cost is continually reduced over time as new pieces of the implementation strategy are put in place. A focused shared-service plan consolidates, then standardizes, in an effort to build customer confidence in service levels while reducing cost.

Consolidating first gets quicker results; savings are realized quickly in short-term efforts that "self-fund" future work. Consolidation also creates a critical mass that helps identify problems, inefficiencies, and interrelationships. There is less resistance this way—top management support is forced because they are really giving up little. It is easier to manage; responsibilities and control of critical functions are clarified.

In the standardization and simplification period, a global data architecture is created and a common business process model and language is deployed, including:

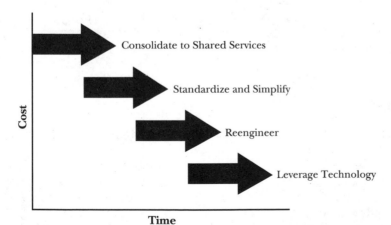

Figure 6-15. Typical shared services implementation strategy.

Standard chart of accounts, with a reduction in the number of accounts and a linkage to detail activities

Standard number schemes for customers, vendors, products, and employees

Direct costing with limited or no allocations and limited or no transfer pricing

There are a number of reasons that finance organizations should start to address shared services as an important ingredient in their overall plans.

First, most financial organizations are upgrading their financial systems; it's a good time to do a top-to-bottom rethinking of how work gets done in the finance organization. Second, reengineering is capturing the imagination of management and consuming staff time. Reengineering the financial organization is important to stay in synch with the rest of the company. Third, going to a shared-service operation is a major change, and after the reengineering wave has rolled through, corporate management may be reluctant to embark on such a major change.

There are a number of risks in not pursuing shared services as a part of the solution: Systems investment could exceed management's expectations while falling short of anticipated benefits. Data architecture will be available to allow world-class management information capabilities, but without shared services the finance organization may not have the time or energy to exploit it.

Establishing shared services will significantly reduce financial operating costs while supporting the redefinition of finance. Finance in the business units will be focused on improving business performance. Shared services will emphasize the operational characteristics of finance. The finance organization will demonstrate commitment to change and delivering results.

Wrap-Up

Bringing your company's processes and systems up to best-practice levels can have a number of benefits, including improved service levels with lower costs and a demonstrated commitment to a new level of partnership. Cutting time and cost out of performing routine transaction processing and fiduciary reporting frees up valuable time and personnel for the value-added analysis the OCFO is increasingly undertaking.

7

Achieving
the
Vision

Now you have a sense of what the best practices are in each of the five imperatives CFOs and their staffs face; integration and partnering, strategy, management control and performance measurement, cost management, and processes and systems. In order to create a holistic vision you need to ask a number of questions.

- Where is my OCFO organization now?
- Where does the OCFO organization need to be in each imperative in order to give the company the ability to remain competitive into the twenty-first century?
- Where should the OCFO organization be in one or two imperatives to help the company become a business or industry leader?
- What is a realistic time frame for making the organizational changes necessary to accomplish this?
- How can the organizational change be managed in such a way as to accomplish its goals and not throw the business and/or the OCFO into chaos while it is going on?

Most companies are really striving to determine their overall priorities and the ways in which they will move forward together. In this effort, strategic clarity is what is most often missing, and this is what truly prevents the organization from moving ahead.

There are often lots of talented and achievement-oriented people within the organization, although there are often also a number of people whose skills no longer fit the organization's needs. Getting rid of them, while unpleasant, is often necessary. People generally understand the business's overall challenges but are loathe to change. Those who populate the finance community often are, by nature, risk averse or risk neutral, and change is a risky proposition.

The key is to get the finance community organized around the new marching orders, the priorities, and a clear sense of where resources should be committed as the effort moves forward. It must be made clear to people that they have to either change or leave; they have to become part of the game plan or go find another place to work. People can't be allowed to "lay in the organizational weeds" and take pot shots at the changes going on.

We believe that fully 70 to 80 percent of activities undertaken in most CFO organizations add little or no value. Of those, about one-quarter are mandated, but three-quarters can be dramatically reduced if not eliminated altogether. In other words, about 60 percent of all of the work done in the OCFO is ripe for internal radical redesign, total elimination, outsourcing, or moving to a shared-service environment to reduce costs and increase efficiency. This frees up time and resources that can be used to focus on those areas that are critical to creating or sustaining competitive advantage.

Remember our OCFO house, seen here again in Figure 7-1.

Think about how over the course of this book we have literally gutted this house and rebuilt it, the same way you would gut and rebuild and modernize a 75-year-old home. Compare the hierarchy in this picture with the hierarchy we have laid out in this book. For instance, in this traditional view, cost management is a bullet point on the second floor of the house—more important than the first-floor transaction processing activities but less important than the strategic management activities, which reside in the penthouse suite. Yet we believe that strategic cost management deserves a chapter unto itself. Strategic cost management is a critical element in the OCFO's quest to add value.

We put all the working-capital management and capital budgeting into the chapter called Strategic Issues—believing that linking all processes to a company's strategic objectives is an integral part of the new world of finance.

We don't see profitability reporting as a strategic issue—reporting is reporting and profitability is generated from other activities that add value. In the converse, order acquisition and procurement can be elevated from mere transactions to value-added activities if done right—by eliminating paperwork, creating vendor and customer relationships

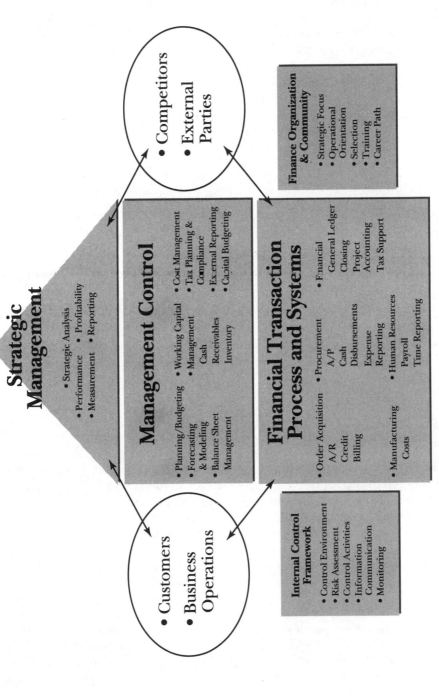

Figure 7-1. The "house" of the OCFO.

with built-in orders and payments, these can become vital short-term cash management tools.

But as we've tried to outline throughout this book, creating the OCFO for the twenty-first century is more than merely moving some of the first-floor activities in Figure 7-1 up to the second floor or vice versa. Creating the new OCFO means challenging assumptions and ways of working, substituting an old mindset of the keeper of the books for a new mindset of the financial creator of value within the strategic and risk-reward parameters defined by executive management.

To do this, the OCFO and the change team must work to achieve six goals:

- Reduce OCFO total cost to less than 1 percent of revenues.
- Simplify and standardize processes to increase their value.
- Consider shared services and outsourcing of routing activities in order to increase time for breakthrough thinking.
- Separate the efficiency-driven back office from the effective business-partnering activities.
- Create a set of roles and responsibilities that promote culture of partnership.
- Address skills and competencies: hire, train, promote, and reward high-quality people who are motivated to change and demonstrate their ability to change.

Positioning, Gaps, and Action Plans

The QuickGrid positioning, distribution, and difficulty graphics we provided in each of the chapters give you an idea of what world class is in each of the critical imperatives, our sense of where the universe of Fortune 1000 companies fall on the position map, and the relative difficulty of moving along the positioning continuum.

In order to create a vision for the OCFO transformation, you need to determine your company's position in each of the imperatives, and discover the gap between your position and world-class companies.

While the agenda of leading OCFOs includes all five major imperatives, it is critical that your vision include an ordering of the imperatives. Your action plan for change should work to improve one or two imperatives at a time—not all simultaneously. A key to this ordering is that it should be based on the importance of each imperative to your company and the potential value in the opportunity. It should not be based merely on the size of the gap between where you are and where you should be.

In other words, you may have already been pushing the organization to excel in the areas most important to the company, although this action was taken on the basis of intuition, rather than through analysis. But many business leaders have good intuition—that's why they have gone as far as they have. Gap size can be misleading.

For instance, Figure 7-2 shows the positioning results of one of our clients. At the end of an assessment, the company determined that it should focus first on improving the financing component of strategy. While the gap between the as-is and the should be is very wide in strategic cost management—the company ranks itself a 2 while best-practice companies are ranked 5, the gap in the area of financing is only one position, between a 2 and a 3. Yet OCFO leadership has determined that reaching best-practice level in procurement and financing can afford the company greater benefit than, say, narrowing the gap in strategic analysis and planning.

Why is this? Because the business was being challenged by one of its greatest customers to enter into joint ventures. In order to do that successfully, the business needed far better currency hedging and capital

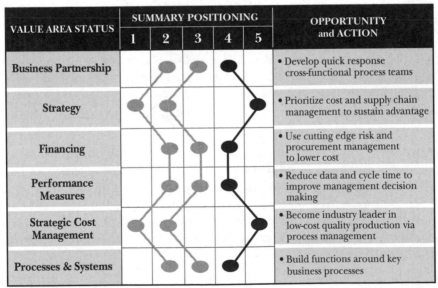

Illustrative Summary Positioning – Company A

VALUE AREA STATUS	SUMMARY POSITIONING					OPPORTUNITY and ACTION
	1	2	3	4	5	
Business Partnership						• Develop quick response cross-functional process teams
Strategy						• Prioritize cost and supply chain management to sustain advantage
Financing						• Use cutting edge risk and procurement management to lower cost
Performance Measures						• Reduce data and cycle time to improve management decision making
Strategic Cost Management						• Become industry leader in low-cost quality production via process management
Processes & Systems						• Build functions around key business processes

Figure 7-2. Representative OCFO positioning results.

sourcing than it ever needed before. The company did not need to be world class, but it certainly needed to be better than a "laggard." It needed to amass new skills quickly, bring in new advisers, and rethink its risk-management policy, or else these joint-venture opportunities would not be viable.

Managing the Change

Our experience shows that unless skillfully implemented, short-term cost-cutting efforts fail to produce sustainable results. Change is not a one-time event, nor is transformation a linear process. True transformational change is dynamic, and it cannot be undertaken in an environment of constant cost cutting. Many variables need to be addressed systematically. To be effective and increase the likelihood of success, your change-management effort must have several key components:

- The desired change must be based on an accepted, common vision that is itself compatible with the company's business objectives.
- There must be senior management leadership, but the day-to-day effort should be driven by line managers. Implementation occurs simultaneously from the top down and from the bottom up.
- Change must be forced through; there is no room for hesitation.
- A critical mass of people must be established who can and will push for the change. Change is highly participative; it needs involvement from all levels, self-implementation, and buy-in by all.
- Honest communication through a well-orchestrated communication plan is the only way. There can be no surprises; surprises lead to distrust and distrust increases resistance to change.
- Do not accept the retention of functional silos; all aspects of the organization must be transformed.
- Involve all people during each stage of the transformation. Ownership and commitment are critical.
- The changes need to be tightly linked to changes in the performance-measurement system and in the reward and compensation system. Individuals need to be measured by their team skills, their business-partnering skills, their communication skills, and their decision-making skills.

There are always choices to be made about how to move through the change process. Sometimes it is sensible to hammer change through quickly; at other times it is better to invest time in constructing the change process carefully in order to minimize the cost of change.

But regardless of the degree of change, change is always difficult and always expensive. As Tom Terez wrote in his classic book, *Modern Management*, "The corporate world is littered with the wreckage of technically sound programs that have been crushed by employee resistance to change."

The costs of change come in many forms. Disruption may only come to light later when the true nature of the cost/benefit equation becomes apparent and executive management commitment to the change fizzles out. Recognizing the high price of major change and knowing when to commit to it is a key skill. Companies must assess the costs, risks, and benefits before undertaking what is often revolutionary change in the CFO organization's orientation, skills, processes, and reward system.

Change management is the process of aligning the organization's people and culture with changes in business strategy, organizational structure, systems, and processes. Properly executed, change management results in:

- Ownership of and commitment to the planned change
- Sustained and measurable improvement
- Improved capability to manage future change

Change Management Requires Insights into People

Managing change requires fundamental insights into how people respond to major change as individuals, as members of small groups, and as members of larger organizations. Within any organization, some people will block change, in various ways and for a variety of reasons. Yet these same people could have been encouraged to support the same change had it been structured differently.

One of the greatest challenges to leadership during an effort to bring about transformational change is to keep the pace, not to settle for complacency and not to set goals and deadlines that are so far in the future that no one will ever know if they are truly met. In fact, because transformation can often be painful, it is clearly better to move associates through the various stages of change as quickly as possible.

Leadership is critical throughout this effort. Corporate leaders and OCFO senior management must address people's natural tendency to resist change. Leadership must create the vision of the desired end state, mobilize the commitment, and insist on the institutionalization of the changes.

On an individual basis, the most dangerous point is what we call *the neutral zone.* This is the period of time when an individual is undergoing a transition and is neither fully withdrawn from the past nor fully committed to the future and the end-state vision. One analogy might be of people escaping a prison through a tunnel. While in the tunnel, there is a natural ambivalence—the prison is bad, but at the other end of the tunnel guards may be waiting with dogs and guns. There may be death. Maybe turning back would be prudent.

It is at this point that many people show their true strength and willingness to change. It is also at this time that leaders need to do a lot of hand-holding, attentive to how each individual is moving through the tunnel and how each individual views both the future viability of the organization and his or her place in it.

Figure 7-3 captures some of the complex individual and organizational dynamics that occur within a trasnformational change, while Figure 7-4 tracks the highs and lows in a typical "Mr. X" as his organization undergoes such a change and he walks through the escape tunnel.

Understanding the risks and opportunities of change is a vital step in taking charge of change. Risks and opportunities are rarely self-evident from the start of a project, but emerge progressively through the life cycle

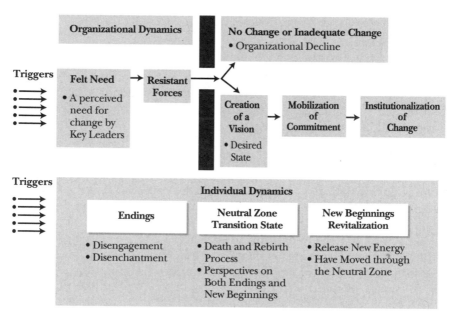

Figure 7-3. Organizational dynamics occurring in the stages of OCFO change.

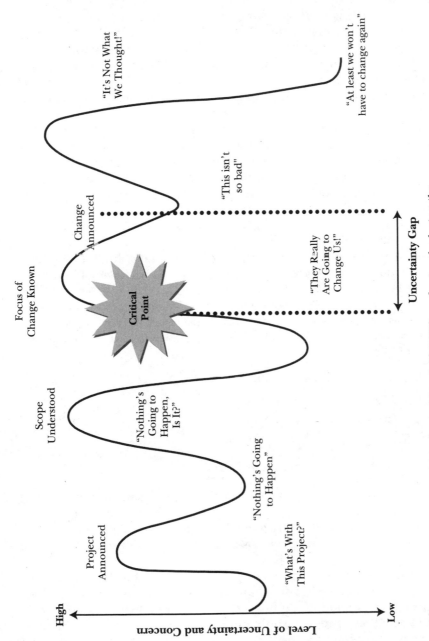

Figure 7-4. Understanding the "highs and lows" of OCFO professionals during the transformation.

of change. Surfacing both the risks and opportunities within any change, and the anxieties these cause, requires continuous diagnosis and discussion between the various sponsors, agents, and targets of the change.

As risks and opportunities become progressively clearer, change processes must be instituted to deal with them. The organization may have to make use of a wide variety of tools and techniques of leadership development, team and technical training, and cultural development to increase its capacity to change, to innovate, and to manage change successfully.

Wherever you start, you must include all the components of transformational change. We assume that there is some pressure for you to change before you embark on this adventure, either from within your organization or from your internal customers and the senior executive team, or perhaps even from outside—analysts, shareholders, or even suppliers. Once you feel pressure for change, our experience shows that the next step is to assess your state of readiness for change and to define organizational imperatives.

Beginning at this time, the organization must rally around and agree upon a model of how it will work in the future. As we have said throughout this book, you must complete both an internal and an external assessment. The external assessment includes benchmarking and comparisons with best-in-class financial organizations and emerging best practices.

When designing a new model of the organization, the OCFO must ask a host of questions:

- Who will we serve as customers?
- What services will we provide?
- How will those services be delivered?
- At what cost will we deliver them?
- What return will we achieve on them?

Regardless of how good the organization believes its own model is, it is critically important to assess where the OCFO's customers believe the organization excels and where it needs improvement. Appendix A has a good set of questions to consider as a starting point when surveying OCFO customers.

Against this model of customer perceptions and business needs, the finance organization must do a hard and honest assessment of its internal positioning and its capabilities. It must determine the organization's true capabilities, and its true commitment to the need for change. (Appendix B has a sample questionnaire you might want to consider adapting to your own organization to get at the perception gaps within the finance organization.)

You need to examine the current process and system capabilities and their associated costs. In this area you must be ruthless in using benchmarking not to give you an answer, but to show you the "art" of the possible. Use the gap between your own capabilities and those of best-practice companies to create the "burning platform" necessary to galvanize within your organization a feeling that change is necessary. Also, use benchmarks as a way for the group to accept targets for cost, head counts, and structure that could differ substantially from today's environment. (See Appendixes C and D for a benchmarking template and for some sample benchmarking results.)

The next item to examine is the constraints that exist to changing the infrastructure, and the constraints that exist to changing the skills and competencies within the staff.

Finally, you must look at the business's challenges, and how this translates into its overall priorities. Is it strategic cost management that will give you the biggest bang for your effort, or is it capital and cash management? Leadership requires the organization to understand how each of its processes support the business's key competitive dimensions.

In Chapter 2, we looked at two companies' vision statements. If you reread that chapter you will see that Johnson & Johnson defined those few areas where it felt its skills could add strategic value to the organization. You cannot be world class in all areas of this new agenda, although we have worked with clients who start out thinking that they can. To be truly world class, you need to find the one or two parts of the new agenda where you need to have a clear-cut strategic advantage and commit yourself to developing and sustaining leadership. Figure 7-5 shows the conclusions that the company cited in Figure 7-2 came to about its priorities.

The company looked not only at its own internal competencies, but where the company as a whole stood against key issues facing it in the future. Out of these the business had decided that three were most critical—global market reach, strategic leverage, and timely product development. When the finance organization considered these priorities as its own, the answer came quite easily—focus on cost management and financing first since there were some major deadlines looming. Then build stronger analytic capabilities in the organization, leveraging off of much of the knowledge that was expected to be generated out of the strategic cost management activity.

After assessment and design comes implementation. This is where you have to put together a detailed design of how the new finance organization will work in terms of the processes, structure, support, people, and rewards. You need to develop a clear migration plan from the current to the future state.

If you have done an honest appraisal of the organization and its customers' needs, you should be more than prepared to make the case to the

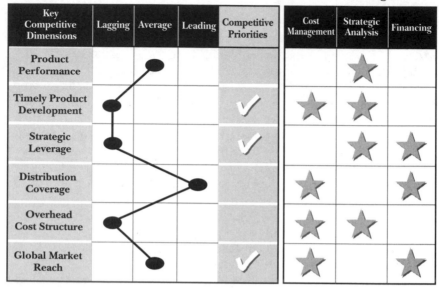

Figure 7-5. OCFO leadership is achieving superior performance that is relevant to the business.

rest of the OCFO on why you are changing. But remember that you have to sell the change both to the OCFO and to its customers, who may be frustrated by some aspects of the current organization but are probably petrified about having to live with changes in the finance organization.

There are several lessons we have learned while helping clients go through this kind of transformational change:

- *Let the people who do the work make the decision.* There is nothing more demoralizing than having someone higher in the hierarchy make decisions or belittle others based on their position. It is a strong leader whose first reaction is "What do you think?"

- *Support people in their efforts!* Do not think of training and information as expenses to be cut. You must be sure that people doing the work are provided with the resources, information access, and continual reinforcement they need. Change requires constant feeding and nourishing.

- *Strive for team-based performance goals.* Set rewards on a team basis.

- *Keep communication focused.* Often, communications are the first to go out the window in the face of lots of activity. Yet communication is the key to success. You must constantly reinforce what behavior is acceptable; you cannot assume people will understand without explanation.

■ *Keep the activities short and focused.* Your greatest rewards are from prototypes and quick deliverables that can be used to get feedback promptly. Remember that you are changing age-old habits ingrained in your staff and in their customers. Learn to reward thinking and improvisation that is aimed at delighting customers. Shed the traditional security of designing, testing ad nauseum, and then implementing on a small basis. Engage your customers; try new things and be ready to kill them if they are not working. Quick deliverables will also help you incrementally adjust the plan to ensure that you are still meeting customer-service levels. You want to get rid of the fat, build up the muscle, and ensure that you are not doing anything to reduce customers' overall service-satisfaction levels.

Finally, after the implementation, you must work to sustain the gains. In many ways, this is the hardest part, not falling back into old behavior patterns and not cutting corners for easy short-term solutions. It is important to develop a dynamic model to support ongoing decision making. Make sure that the model explains the purpose and need for each function and process in the "new" organization as it relates to the overall company strategy.

Are You Ready to Change?

Successful change requires understanding not only how to change an organization, but whether the organization is ready for change. Success will only come if six key areas are in balance:

■ Vision and leadership

■ Need

■ Structured process

■ Capacity and resources

■ Measurement and rewards

■ Communications

Vision and Leadership. To transform an OCFO organization, a company must develop and agree upon a vision that encompasses the role and contribution expected from the OCFO, the core processes and systems, the control framework, and the manner in which the contribution is in line with the entire organization's culture.

Need for Change. The need for change must be compelling and well established. Executive management must be committed to the change and widely communicate the change throughout the organization.

Structured Processes. These are necessary to identify some early wins, to gain momentum, and to solidify advocates for change behind the effort. Appropriate teams need to be identified; detailed plans and communication strategies and plans need to be developed.

Capacity and Resources. To engage in a successful change, the OCFO must look at its vision carefully and scrutinize the implications for its new requirements and resources. Existing resources must be matched where there is a need. Where there are excesses of ill-fitting resources, management must aggressively and consistently provide training and coaching. For those who cannot develop the necessary skills, management must not be loath to recognize the need for some people to leave the organization.

Measurement and Rewards. Measures must be reviewed and changed, but then management must continually strive to understand if the measures and reward systems are changing behavior in the intended ways. Communicating these changes back to the staff and the rest of the organization are important to defining, implementing, and solidifying the new measures.

Communications. Finally, the communications strategy must reinforce the new objectives, vision, and measures. Only when people understand how they are expected to live up to the new objectives, vision, and measures will they behave in accordance with them.

Appendix A

Interview Guide for Finance Customers

Discuss the role of the OCFO as supplier and partner

Strategic Management

1. Describe the role of the finance organization in assessing your business unit's contribution to economic value. How does the finance organization participate in the construction of planning models reflecting your business unit's value chain and value drivers?

2. Does the finance organization support your business unit in linking strategy with implementation? How?

3. For a typical operations or marketing activity run by your unit, can you describe two examples of how the finance organization has added value to your business? Can you think of two areas where you wish you had more finance organization involvement?

4. To what extent are financial information systems modeled to collect and structure information in terms of account and customer profitability, and how is that information used for strategic management?

5. Discuss the manner in which your business unit uses financial organization resources to:

   Assess strategic investments
   Frame competitive analyses

Management Control

1. What is the extent and value of finance organization staff knowledge of the business and operational experiences?

2. How relevant are the operational performance measures in tracking your business unit's financial and nonfinancial value drivers and gauging the achievement of business objectives?

    For example: Are the performance measurements identifying information that is predictive and actionable? How well does the performance measurement process measure what is important to your customers? How well does the performance measurement process motivate toward continuous improvement?

3. Does the performance planning process reflect the professed business unit vision and strategic goals reflected in the budget? Are strategy and goals constantly communicated to all levels of the unit or are they communicated only at budget time?

Business Processes

1. How integrated are finance organization processes, priorities, and imperatives with those of your business unit?

    For example: Are financial systems adapted to operational drivers or are financial imperatives attempting to drive the structure of operational decisions? How flexible is the finance organization in meeting your business unit's changing needs? Overall, would you say the finance organization serving your business unit is more process-focused or bottom-line/numbers-focused?

2. How effectively are financial controls built into your unit's business processes?

    For example: Who has responsibility for these controls...finance or operations people? Are financial controls evaluated in terms of their cost benefits and relationships to business objectives or in terms of their effectiveness in achieving financial reporting objectives? How effective have these controls been at preventing undesirable risk?

3. Do you have a sense that your finance organization is aware of and working to incorporate cutting-edge financial and business information processes pioneered outside the company?

4. In your business unit, do finance-oriented process and technology value assessments tend to come more from the customers' perspective or from concrete measurements of productivity and cost?

5. From your perspective, what is the CFO's primary role in supporting your business unit's operations? How would you like to see that role evolve?

Activities & Cost Management

1. From your perspective, is your finance organization more concerned with managing costs relative to value or simply cutting costs?

   For example: Does your finance organization cost by activity (value added versus nonvalue added)? Does your finance organization cost by product? Does your finance organization cost by value chain (i.e., profitability by/of market segment, customer, geography)? How are the value of activity or project results analyzed relative to costs?

2. Describe initiatives your business unit has taken to manage costs. Describe the role the finance organization has played in these initiatives.

   Areas in which initiatives might be taken would include overhead, product development, support category management, segment management, and operations management

Appendix B
Finance Alignment Survey

Please read the following statements *as they pertain to your company's finance organization.* In the first set of columns indicate the extent to which you agree or disagree with the statement. In the second set of columns indicate the priority you would assign to improving the issue over the next year.

	Disagree			Agree		Not a priority			Top priority	
Strategic Management										
My finance organization:										
Makes accurate financial assumptions in corporate and business unit strategic planning processes.	1	2	3	4	5	1	2	3	4	5
Actively assesses the contribution of the business to our overall performance.	1	2	3	4	5	1	2	3	4	5
Effectively participates in the development of business unit planning models that reflect the business' key drivers of value and competitive environment.	1	2	3	4	5	1	2	3	4	5

	Disagree					Agree					Not a priority					Top priority			

Strategic Management

My finance organization:

Commits an ongoing effort
to confirming the accuracy of its
strategic planning assumptions.
1 2 3 4 5   1 2 3 4 5

Brings ideas to our business
units that add value.
1 2 3 4 5   1 2 3 4 5

Is focused on realizing the
organization's business
objectives.
1 2 3 4 5   1 2 3 4 5

Actively serves on cross-
functional teams with the
business units.
1 2 3 4 5   1 2 3 4 5

Assists management in
measuring its performance
against the approved strategy
and operating plans.
1 2 3 4 5   1 2 3 4 5

Performs analyses of strategic
investments that are regularly
used to make investment
decisions.
1 2 3 4 5   1 2 3 4 5

Plays a key role in developing
competitive analyses for the
business.
1 2 3 4 5   1 2 3 4 5

Performance Measurement & Management Control

My finance organization:

Understands the financial and
operational key drivers of
performance and integrates
these in its management
reporting process.
1 2 3 4 5   1 2 3 4 5

Adds value through its
management reporting.
1 2 3 4 5   1 2 3 4 5

Tracks and analyzes information
that is predictive and actionable.
1 2 3 4 5   1 2 3 4 5

Measures what is important.
1 2 3 4 5   1 2 3 4 5

Tracks and analyzes information
that is motivated toward
continuous improvement in our
processes.
1 2 3 4 5   1 2 3 4 5

	Disagree			Agree		Not a priority			Top priority	
Performance Measurement & Management Control											

My finance organization:

	Disagree			Agree		Not a priority			Top priority	
Incorporates measures of competitor status into management reports.	1	2	3	4	5	1	2	3	4	5
Coordinates a budget and planning process that reflects the business unit vision and strategic goals.	1	2	3	4	5	1	2	3	4	5
Communicates performance goals and strategy to all levels of the unit throughout the year (not just at budget time).	1	2	3	4	5	1	2	3	4	5
Uses too much detail in the performance planning and budgeting process than is necessary to achieve overall vision and strategic goals.	1	2	3	4	5	1	2	3	4	5
Makes sure that the business performance plans and individual performance are aligned through incentive structures, recognition, training, and career planning.	1	2	3	4	5	1	2	3	4	5
Shares with operations accountability for the delivery of agreed-upon performance.	1	2	3	4	5	1	2	3	4	5

Business Processes & Systems											

My finance organization:

	Disagree			Agree		Not a priority			Top priority	
Is more bottom-line/numbers-focused than process-focused.	1	2	3	4	5	1	2	3	4	5
Effectively builds financial controls into business processes.	1	2	3	4	5	1	2	3	4	5
Develops the responsibility for controls with the business units.	1	2	3	4	5	1	2	3	4	5
Evaluates controls more in terms of their relationship to business objectives than their effectiveness in achieving financial reporting objectives.	1	2	3	4	5	1	2	3	4	5
Deploys financial controls that are effective at preventing undesirable risk.	1	2	3	4	5	1	2	3	4	5

	Disagree					Not a priority			Top priority	
Business Processes & Systems										

My finance organization:

Is flexible, adapting its processes to meet the business' changing needs.	1	2	3	4	5	1	2	3	4	5
Aligns its processes and priorities with those of the business units.	1	2	3	4	5	1	2	3	4	5
Quickly adapts financial systems to operational requirements and business needs.	1	2	3	4	5	1	2	3	4	5
Is aware of and working to incorporate cutting-edge financial and business processes pioneered outside the company.	1	2	3	4	5	1	2	3	4	5
Is using information technology to facilitate the integration of financial and operating systems.	1	2	3	4	5	1	2	3	4	5
Makes process and technology value assessments from the customer's perspective.	1	2	3	4	5	1	2	3	4	5
Plays an up-front and early role in most product decision-making processes.	1	2	3	4	5	1	2	3	4	5
Supports the development of customer and operational systems to adapt to changing customer requirements.	1	2	3	4	5	1	2	3	4	5
Has been systematically redesigning or eliminating costly financial control /tracking activities.	1	2	3	4	5	1	2	3	4	5
Strives to reduce the cycle time between an event and feedback.	1	2	3	4	5	1	2	3	4	5

Activity and Cost Management										

My finance organization:

Works with the business units to reduce the non-value-added costs in their operations.	1	2	3	4	5	1	2	3	4	5
Is more concerned with managing costs relative to value rather than simply cutting costs.	1	2	3	4	5	1	2	3	4	5

	Disagree	Agree	Not a priority	Top priority

Activity and Cost Management

My finance organization:

Understands the long-term cost structure of our business.	1 2 3 4 5	1 2 3 4 5
Supports the business with reliable product cost information.	1 2 3 4 5	1 2 3 4 5
Supports the business with reliable customer cost information.	1 2 3 4 5	1 2 3 4 5
Supports the business with reliable market segment cost information.	1 2 3 4 5	1 2 3· 4 5
Analyzes the value of activity or project results relative to costs.	1 2 3 4 5	1 2 3 4 5
Is knowledgeable about activity-based management concepts.	1 2 3 4 5	1 2 3 4 5
Is skilled in activity-based management analyses.	1 2 3 4 5	1 2 3 4 5

Organization Structure & Skills

My finance organization:

Actively works as a business partner with our customers.	1 2 3 4 5	1 2 3 4 5
Is considered a business partner by its customers.	1 2 3 4 5	1 2 3 4 5
Is business advocate rather than corporate policeman.	1 2 3 4 5	1 2 3 4 5
Puts a high priority on learning.	1 2 3 4 5	1 2 3 4 5
Has responsibility to make change happen.	1 2 3 4 5	1 2 3 4 5
Promotes sharing between groups.	1 2 3 4 5	1 2 3 4 5
Responds quickly to customers.	1 2 3 4 5	1 2 3 4 5
Encourages the use of cross-functional teams.	1 2 3 4 5	1 2 3 4 5
Encourages me to learn new ideas and tools.	1 2 3 4 5	1 2 3 4 5
Seeks new ways to complete our work.	1 2 3 4 5	1 2 3 4 5

How long have you been with the company? _____

How long have you been in your current position? _____

What is your current position? _____

Appendix C
How to Start Your Benchmarking Effort

To start your benchmarking, you need to collect key information on staffing levels, costs, and transaction volume for key business processes in the office of the CFO at your company. To the extent possible, the data that you collect should reflect the actual results from your last completed fiscal year.

To start the data collection effort, follow the steps outlined below:

- Identify the organizations to be reported in the study.

- Identify a contact person within the corporate financial organization to coordinate all of the data collection and analysis.

- Identify a local finance contact person(s) within each of the business units to coordinate all of the data collection.

- Send each of the contacts a copy of the instructions so they can become familiar with the requirements.

- Schedule a telephone conference call with all contacts to explain the purpose of this effort and to review the activities to be undertaken. (This first call usually takes 1 to 2 hours.)

- Establish dates for visiting each site and for completing the data collection.

Each of the business unit coordinators should be ready to verify that the head count and cost data "foots" or reasonably matches the actual expenses and that any allocations for systems and other costs do not lead to "double counting" of expenses at the summary level.

During the effort consider holding regularly scheduled conference calls that are open to any of the business unit coordinators. The purpose of these calls is to communicate information about the data collection effort, respond to questions and issues in order to ensure data consistency, and monitor progress.

Step 1: Understand the Definitions of Processes to Be Studied

In any benchmarking exercise, it is important to understand just what is truly being benchmarked. Many of the sources of benchmarking information may have slightly different definitions of the processes, so it is critical to understand what each one means by a process, what is included and what is not. While your organization's own definitions may differ from those of an outside benchmarking source, we would strongly urge you to try to conform the data collection effort to those of the outside source in order to ensure more comparability of the results.

To give you an idea of how we at Coopers & Lybrand have defined some of the processes, we present below the definitions which we often use as a starting point. If you are collecting information for your own purposes, feel free to use these as a guide.

- *Accounts Payable:* Transactions designed to record, verify, and pay vendor invoices. This includes the matching of orders to invoices, the development of any required adjustments, the processing and entry of transactions into the appropriate systems, and the monitoring and reporting of these transactions.

- *Accounts Receivable:* Transactions designed to record, verify, and track balances due from customers who have received goods and services from the company. This process includes the verification and analysis of customer balances, the entry of remittances received, and the preparation of required aging or other management reports.

- *Budgeting and Performance Planning:* Activities which result in the development of short-term (12 to 18 month) financial plans and budgets. This activity includes the definition of budgetary guidelines, the management of the budgeting process for the company, the development of any finance department period cost projections, the consolidation of business unit submissions, and the development of consolidated corporate views of the budget.

- *Collection:* Transactions designed to collect outstanding balances from customers for services or products delivered by the company. This process includes the use of any external collection agencies to assist in the collection of delinquent account balances.

- *Cost Accounting:* Activities to determine the cost structure of specific activities, products, or services conducted by the company. This process also involves activities that involve the definition of the conceptual framework for cost attribution and allocation as well as the analysis on variances of actual costs against any predetermined standards.

- *Credit Management:* Transactions designed to review requests by customers for credit as well as the extension of this credit. This process involves developing credit policies, analyzing credit requests through both internal and external data sources, approving those requests that are consistent with corporate policies, and working with the operations and field organizations of the company to communicate the decisions back to the customers.

- *Customer Billing:* Transactions designed to issue bills to customers for products or services delivered by the company as well as to record the associated revenue. This process includes the collection of required billing information, the calculation of appropriate billing amounts for goods, services, and related taxes, the entry and production of bills from automated or manual billing systems, the distribution of bills to the customers, and the reporting on billing balances to management.

- *Fixed Assets/Property:* Transactions designed to record and control the capital assets on the balance sheet of the company including their acquisition, disposition, depreciation, and transfer. This activity also includes the physical verification of assets periodically conducted by the company. This process includes tracking asset values for both book and tax purposes.

- *General Accounting:* Activities that maintain and control the accounting records of the company as well as any business units. Specific activities included in this process are the updating and maintenance of the general ledger, the reconciliation of any ledger balances, the closing of the books, and the regular preparation of standard financial reports. Also included in this process is the preparation of all required statutory or regulatory reports required by external constituents of the company including, but not limited to, the SEC, stockholders, government entities, regulatory entities.

- *Internal Audit and Controls:* Activities designed to ensure that the controls of the company are effective and in compliance with required standards. This process includes the development of control policies, the completion of internal operating and financial reviews, and the reporting to management on the adequacy of the controls as well as any recommendations for improvement. This process also includes supporting a regular recurring audit undertaken by an external third party on behalf of the company.

- *Inventory Accounting:* Transactions designed to record and value the inventories of the company. The inventories included in this process are the raw material, work in progress, and finished goods inventories.

- *Management Reporting:* Activities designed to evaluate financial and operational information that reflects the drivers of business performance. The focus of this process includes both consolidated company-wide views as well as any business unit specific analyses or evaluations conducted by the office of the CFO. This process also includes the evaluation of proposed decisions for management including acquisitions, dispositions, new product development, and pricing structures.

- *Office of the CFO Administrative Support:* The individuals involved in this process should be limited to the administrative support staff for senior financial executives who establish policies and manage the activities of other functional and process managers in the finance function.

- *Office of the CFO Management:* The individuals involved in this process should be limited to senior financial executives. These individuals establish policies and manage the activities of other functional and process managers in the finance function.

- *Payroll:* Activities of planning, recording, monitoring, and reporting on wages and benefits paid to employees of the company. The activities in this process are limited to the payment of wages, benefits and pensions paid to employees, and the accounting for benefit plans required by the company's policies. The activities included in the process start with the entry of time records into the payroll systems and end with the reporting on payments to employees, management, and the government.

- *Risk Management:* Activities designed to plan, administer, record, and report on the actual and potential financial effect of losses incurred by the company through claims or loss of assets. The process includes the evaluation of alternative risk scenarios, the development of a corporate risk strategy as well as any related negotiations of third-party insurance coverage that is called for in the strategy.

- *Tax Planning and Compliance:* Activities designed to plan, report, and record/comply on the tax liabilities of the company. The process includes compiling tax information and filing the appropriate compliance forms with local, state, and federal agencies. The process also includes researching and evaluating alternative approaches to complying with income, property, employee, and sales and use taxes that are designed to optimize the company's tax position and financial effectiveness. Advising management of tax-related issues as well as conducting any required tax audits and litigation-related evaluations is also included.

- *Travel and Expense Processing:* Disbursements of cash advances as well as all transactions designed to record, verify, and pay reimbursement claims for expenses incurred on behalf of the corporation.

- *Treasury and Cash Management:* Activities designed to plan, record, and report on the cash flow and investment requirements of the company. The activities of the process include the management of relationships with external banks and investment advisers as well as the evaluation of their performance, the establishment and control of depository and investment accounts, the forecasting of operating cash requirements, the management of any foreign currency activities, and the execution of any required financing activities. Also included is the development of a corporate treasury and investment strategy and any associated evaluations of financing alternatives to ensure consistency with this strategy.

Step 2: Gather the Expense and Cost Data

The expense and cost data requires that you analyze the costs for each of the distinct processes undertaken by the finance function in terms of their composition in three broad categories—personnel related, information technology/systems related, and other. As you look at these, try to also break them down in terms of the direct costs managed by the finance function as well as those which are charged via overhead allocations or transfer costs from other parts of the organization. Making the distinction is important to ensure that you do not double-count.

The three categories of costs follow the classifications that we have found to be readily available in many of the finance organizations with whom Coopers & Lybrand works. Guidelines for completing the form completely and consistently with the other survey participants are as follows:

- *Direct expenses* are those which are charged and recorded on the OCFO's books.

- The direct personnel-related costs should be consistent with the head count figures you will use.

- *Allocated expenses* are those which are incurred by another portion of the organization and which are charged to your organization.

Step 3: Gather Process-Volume and Transaction Data

Step 3 requires you to gather a variety of specific metrics for each process, including indicators of volume, timeliness, dollar value, and processing accuracy.

From our experience with previous benchmarking efforts, we know that this part of the survey is generally the hardest to complete because the data often reside within individual processing or transaction units. As a result, to complete this section most survey participants will find that they must reach out to many different parts of the finance function to obtain the required data and to make specific data requests from the records of the transaction systems themselves.

Step 4: Gather Head Count Data

The head count data that you need to gather can usually be completed using your payroll and human resources records. The following guidelines should ensure that the data are complete and consistent:

- Head count should be included on the basis of full-time equivalents (FTEs). Include all open positions in the head count numbers.

- Part time employees should also be converted to an FTE basis. If you have employees who work 20 hours per week, their FTE equivalent is 0.5. For example, if you have a staff member who works a total of 20 hours per week out of a 40-hour standard workweek and splits this time evenly between accounts payable and time & expense processing, the employee's time should be included as 0.25 FTE in accounts payable and 0.25 to time & expense.

In some companies where many staff members perform a variety of functions, it may be easier to get each individual person or supervisor to estimate how work is distributed among the various processes identified on the form. If you decide to proceed in this manner, we recommend that you copy the form, distribute it to the employees or supervisors, and ask them to estimate how they spend their time on average. Keep estimates in 10 percent increments. When you receive the worksheets from the individuals, total all the percentages for an activity and convert the total to an FTE basis: e.g., a total of 650 percent is recorded for accounts receivable or 6.5 FTEs.

Your staffing levels should be broken down into four major categories as follows:

- *Management employees* for the purposes of this survey are those employees who are primarily responsible for managing a group of staff in terms of planning, operations oversight, and administrative compliance.

- *Other exempt employees* are those employees who generally perform accounting and finance functions that are either analytical or technical. These employees are not eligible for overtime. They may be either full-time or part-time.

- *Nonexempt employees* are those employees who perform the data entry, production, or other administrative functions. These employees are generally classified as nonexempt and are typically eligible for overtime.

- *Temporary/contract employees* are those staff resources which are regularly utilized to complete an activity or process. These resources generally are accounted for separately and are not on the payroll of the company directly. They may be either full-time or part-time. They may be obtained through either a temporary staffing agency or through a contractual services contract. In all cases the company does not pay for benefits for these resources. While we recognize that obtaining an estimate of these resources may be difficult as they are often brought in to assist in processing during temporarily high activity levels, it is our experience that temporary and contract employees are becoming an increasingly important segment of a company's overall resource profile. Therefore, we suggest that you develop an estimate of the regular temporary/contract resources by process.

Step 5: Calculate Your Metrics

The last step is to put the data which you have collected into a spreadsheet and calculate your own benchmark metrics. Samples of the three spreadsheets which we use as our starting point are shown on the following pages.

Finally, once you have organized all of your data it is time to calculate some metrics. While the list below may not be exhaustive, it does represent the core of what most outside benchmarking organizations collect and can provide to you.

Accounts Payable

- Cost per invoice
- Labor cost per invoice
- Number of invoices processed per FTE
- Number of supplier queries/complaints last year as % of # of invoices
- Number of transaction errors per year as % of # of invoices
- Percent of invoices paid electronically
- Percent of transactions covered with blanket PO
- Personnel cost as % of total process cost
- Systems cost as a % of total process cost
- Process cost as % of total OCFO costs
- Process cost as % of revenue
- Staff per $100 million in sales (or $1 billion)

Travel and Entertainment Processing

- Cost per T&E processed
- Labor cost per expense report
- Number of expense reports filed per employee
- Number of expense reports processed per T&E FTE
- Percentage of T&E reimbursement claims direct deposited
- Personnel cost as % of total process cost
- Systems cost as a % of total process cost
- Process cost as % of total OCFO costs
- Process cost as % of Revenue
- Staff per $100 million in sales (or $1 billion)

Accounts Receivable

- Accounts receivable turnover (sales/average accounts receivable)
- Days sales outstanding
- Cost per remittance
- Labor cost per remittance
- Number of remittances processed per FTE
- Percentage of remittances handled electronically

- Personnel cost as % of total process cost
- Systems cost as a % of total process cost
- Process cost as % of total OCFO costs
- Process cost as % of revenue
- Staff per $100 million in sales

Collection and Credit Management

- Write-offs as a percent of net sales
- Cost per credit approval
- Cost per credit review
- Number of accounts per credit and collection FTE
- Number of credit reviews per credit FTE
- Personnel cost as % of total process cost
- Systems cost as a % of total process cost
- Process cost as % of total OCFO costs
- Process cost as % of revenue
- Staff per $100 million in sales (or $1 billion)

Customer Billing

- Number of customer inquiries/complaints last year as % of # bills issued
- Labor cost per bill issued
- Number of bills issued per FTE
- Personnel cost as % of total process cost
- Systems cost as a % of total process cost
- Process cost as % of total OCFO costs
- Process cost as % of revenue
- Staff per $100 million in sales (or $1 billion)

Fixed Assets/Property

- Cost per asset records processed
- Asset records processed per fixed asset FTE
- Number of assets tracked per FTE
- Personnel cost as % of total process cost

- Systems cost as a % of total process cost
- Process cost as % of total OCFO costs
- Process cost as % of revenue
- Staff per $100 million in sales (or $1 billion)

General Ledger

- Intercompany transactions as a percent of total transactions
- Average number of days required to close the books
- Percent of journal vouchers manually generated
- Number of journal vouchers per general accounting FTE
- Average cost per # journal voucher (annual cost/journal voucher)
- Personnel cost as % of total process cost
- Systems cost as a % of total process cost
- Process cost as % of total OCFO costs
- Process cost as % of revenue
- Staff per $100 million in sales (or $1 billion)

Financial Function Management

- Overall costs per CFO employee ($000)
- Finance cost as % of revenue—personnel
- Finance cost as % of revenue—systems
- Finance cost as % of revenue—other
- Finance cost as % of revenue
- Finance staff as percent of total employment
- Finance staff per $100 million in revenue (or $1 billion)
- Number of finance contract head count as percent of total finance head count
- Number of finance exempt head count as percent of total finance head count
- Number of finance nonexempt head count as percent of total finance head count

Payroll/Benefits

- Labor cost per check

- Labor cost per employee
- Systems cost per check
- Systems cost per employee
- Total cost per check
- Total cost per employee paid
- Number of employees per time and attendance FTE
- Number of paychecks per FTE
- Percent of paychecks with direct deposit—exempt employees
- Percent of paychecks with direct deposit—nonexempt employees
- Personnel cost as % of total process cost
- Systems cost as a % of total process cost
- Process cost as % of total OCFO costs
- Process cost as % of revenue
- Staff per $100 million in sales (or $1 billion)

Tax Planning and Compliance

- Percent of returns amended
- Percent of returns automated
- Number of returns per compliance FTE
- Personnel cost as a % of total process cost
- Systems cost as a % of total process cost
- Process cost as % of total OCFO costs
- Process cost as % of revenue
- Staff per $100 million in sales (or $1 billion)

Inventory Management

- Days of inventory outstanding ((average inventory/COGS)×360)
- Cost per line items (SKUs) tracked
- Number of line items (SKUs) tracked per FTE
- Personnel cost as % of total process cost
- Systems cost as a % of total process cost
- Process cost as % of total OCFO costs
- Process cost as % of revenue

- Staff per $100 million in sales (or $1 billion)

Treasury/Cash Management

- Manual wires as a percentage of total wires
- Standing wires as a percentage of total wires
- Personnel cost as a % of total process cost
- Systems cost as a % of total process cost
- Process cost as % of total OCFO costs
- Process cost as % of revenue
- Staff per $100 million in sales (or $1 billion)

Management Reporting

- Personnel cost as % of total process cost
- Systems cost as a % of total process cost
- Process cost as % of total OCFO costs
- Process cost as % of revenue
- Staff per $100 million in sales (or $1 billion)

Budget/Performance Planning

- Length of formal budgeting process (in weeks)
- Personnel cost as % of total process cost
- Systems cost as a % of total process cost
- Process cost as % of total OCFO costs
- Process cost as % of revenue
- Staff per $100 million in sales (or $1 billion)

Appendix D
Illustrative Benchmarking Data

Representative General Accounting Metrics

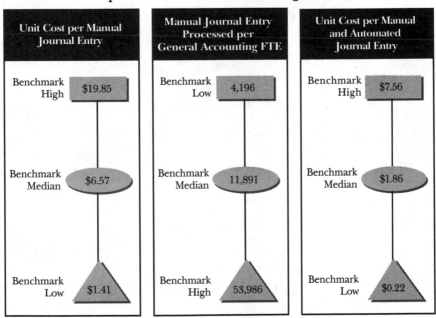

Source: Continuous Improvement Center, Institute of Management Accountants, 1995.

Chart 1. Representative general accounting metrics.

Representative Payroll Metrics

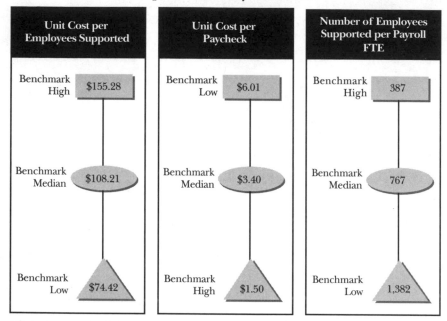

Source: Continuous Improvement Center, Institute of Management Accountants, 1995.

Chart 2. Representative payroll metrics.

Representative Accounts Payable Metrics

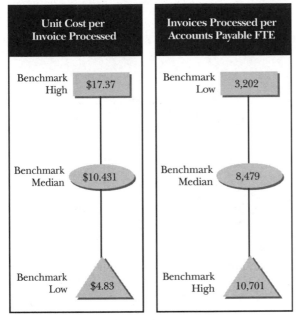

Source: Continuous Improvement Center,
      Institute of Management Accountants, 1995.

Chart 3. Representative accounts payable metrics.

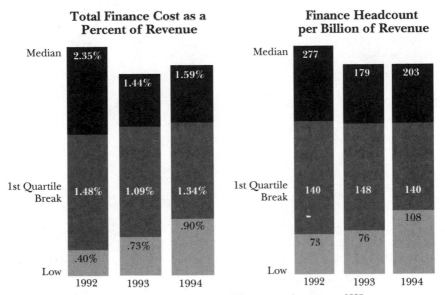

Source: Continuous Improvement Center, Institute of Management Accountants, 1995.

Chart 4. (a) Total finance cost as a percent of revenue. (b) Finance head count per billion of revenue.

Bibliography

Baldwin, Y. C., and K. B. Clark, 1992, "Capabilities and Capital Investment: New Perspectives on Capital Budgeting," *Journal of Applied Corporate Finance,* 5, 2.

Bennis, Warren, 1989, *On Becoming a Leader,* Reading, MA: Addison-Wesley.

Carr, David K., and Henry J. Johansson, 1995, *Best Practices in Reengineering,* New York: McGraw-Hill.

Collins, James C., and Jerry Porras, 1994, *Built to Last: Successful Habits of Visionary Companies,* New York: HarperCollins.

Cooper, Robin, 1995, *When Lean Enterprises Collide,* Boston: Harvard Business School Press.

————, 1989, "You Need a New Cost System When...," *Harvard Business Review,* 67, 1.

Davidow, William H., and Michael S. Malone, 1992, *The Virtual Corporation: Structuring and Revitalizing the Corporation for the 21st Century,* New York: HarperBusiness.

Day, George S., and Liam Fahey, "Putting Strategy into Shareholder Value Analysis," *Harvard Business Review,* March–April 1990.

Dixit, Avinash K., and Barry J. Nalebuff, 1991, *Thinking Strategically: The Competitive Edge in Business, Politics and Everyday Life,* New York: W. W. Norton.

Donaldson, Gordon, 1994, *Corporate Restructuring: Managing the Change Process From Within,* Boston: Harvard Business Press.

Hamel, Gary, and C. K. Prahalad, 1994, *Competing for the Future,* Boston: Harvard Business School Press.

Hammer, Michael, and James Champy, 1993, *Reengineering the Corporation: A Manifesto for Business Revolution,* New York: HarperBusiness.

Hofer, Charles W., and Dan Schendel, 1978, *Strategy Formulation: Analytical Concepts,* St. Paul, MN: West Publishing.

Johnson, H. Thomas, and Robert S. Kaplan, 1987, *Relevance Lost: The Rise and Fall of Management Accounting,* Boston: Harvard Business School.

Kanter, Rosabeth Moss, 1991, "Championing Change: An Interview with Bell Atlantic's CEO Raymond Smith," *Harvard Business Review,* 69, 1.

————, 1989, *When Giants Learn to Dance: Mastering the Challenge of Strategy, Management and Careers in the 1990's,* New York: Simon and Schuster.

Kaplan, Robert S., and Robin Cooper, 1988. "Get Your Costs Right," *Harvard Business Review,* 66, 5.

Kaplan, Robert S., and David Norton, 1992, "The Balanced Scorecard—Measures that Drive Performance," *Harvard Business Review,* 70, 1.

Knight, Charles F., "Emerson Electric: Consistent Profits, Consistently," *Harvard Business Review,* January–February 1992.

McTaggart, James M., Peter W. Kontes, and Michael C. Mankins, 1994, *The Value Imperative: Managing for Superior Shareholder Returns*, New York: The Free Press.

Porter, Michael, 1985, *Competitive Advantage: Creating and Sustaining Superior Performance*, New York: The Free Press.

———, 1980, *Competitive Strategy: Techniques for Analyzing Industries and Competitors*, New York: The Free Press.

Prahalad, C. K., and Gary Hamel, 1990, "The Core Competence of the Corporation," *Harvard Business Review*, 68, 3.

Quinn, James B., 1992, *Intelligent Enterprise: A Knowledge and Service Based Paradigm for Industry*, New York: The Free Press.

———, 1980, *Strategies for Change: Logical Incrementalism*. Homewood, IL: Richard D. Irwin.

Rappaport, Alfred, 1987, "Linking Competitive Strategy and Shareholder Value Analysis," *The Journal of Business Strategy*, 7, 4.

———, 1986, *Creating Shareholder Value*, New York: The Free Press.

Rommel, Gunter, Jurgen Kluge, Rolf-Dieter Kempis, Raimund Diederichs, and Felix Bruck, 1995, *Simplicity Wins: How Germany's Mid-Sized Industrial Companies Succeed*, Boston: Harvard School Business Press.

Shank, John K. and Vijay Govindarajan, 1993, *Strategic Cost Management: The New Tool for Competitive Advantage*, New York: The Free Press.

———, 1989, *Strategic Cost Analysis*, Homewood, IL: Richard D. Irwin.

———, 1988, " Making Strategy Explicit in Cost Analysis: A Case Study," *Sloan Management Review*, 29, 3.

Simons, Robert, 1995, *Levers of Control: How Managers Use Innovative Control Systems to Drive Strategic Renewal*, Boston: Harvard Business School Press.

Stalk, George, Philip Evans and Lawrence E. Shulman," Competing on Capabilities: The New Rules of Corporate Strategy," *Harvard Business Review*, March–April 1992.

Stewart, G. Bennett III, 1991, *The Quest for Value*, New York: Harper Business.

Tichy, Noel, and Stratford Sherman, 1993, *Control Your Destiny or Someone Else Will: How Jack Welch is Making General Electric the World's Most Competitive Corporation*, New York: Doubleday.

Waldrop, M. Mitchell, 1992, *Complexity: The Emerging Science at the Edge of Order and Chaos*, New York: Simon & Schuster.

Willigan, Geraldine E., "The Value Adding CFO: An Interview with Gary Wilson," *Harvard Business Review*, January–February 1990.

Index

About the Authors

THOMAS F. WALTHER is a Partner with Coopers & Lybrand Consulting. His career with Coopers & Lybrand for more than twenty years has focused on improving the effectiveness of the financial function across a variety of industries. This focus culminated in his having national responsibility for developing Coopers & Lybrand's Office of the CFO Practice. He now focuses these efforts within the Information and Telecommunications Industry Group. He lives in Stamford, CT.

HENRY J. JOHANSSON is a Partner with Coopers & Lybrand Consulting in the Information and Telecommunications Industry Group. His career with Coopers & Lybrand began in 1976 with a focus on performance improvement for manufacturers. This led to his responsibility for Coopers & Lybrand's U.S. Manufacturing Industry Practice. He has coauthored three books dealing with business process reengineering, the latest entitled *Best Practices in Reengineering: What Works and What Doesn't in the Reengineering Process.* He lives in Fort Lee, NJ.

JOHN R. DUNLEAVY is also a Partner with Coopers & Lybrand Consulting. After a short period as a member of the Business Assurance and Auditing staff, he moved into the consulting practice where he worked in the areas of financial management, process analysis, and cost management. Over the last twenty years he has primarily focused on issues of organizational performance and financial management in the Information and Telecommunications Industries. He lives in Greenwich, CT.

ELIZABETH HJELM began her career with Coopers & Lybrand Consulting in 1982 with a focus on marketing and financial information systems. Prior to her departure, she was a member of the Information and Telecommunications Industry Group where she was involved in performance measurement, strategic analysis, planning, and financial transaction processes reengineering projects. She now resides in Wilton, CT.